Church Conflict

The Hidden Systems Behind the Fights

Charles H. Cosgrove &
Dennis D. Hatfield

Abingdon Press
Nashville

CHURCH CONFLICT: THE HIDDEN SYSTEMS BEHIND THE FIGHTS

Copyright © 1994 by Abingdon Press

This book is printed on acid-free, recycled paper.

Library of Congress Cataloging-in-Publication Data

Cosgrove, Charles H.
  Church conflict: the hidden system behind the fights / Charles H. Cosgrove and Dennis D. Hatfield.
      p.   cm.
  Includes bibliographical references.
  ISBN 0-687-08152-1 (alk. paper)
    1. Church controversies. 2. Family psychotherapy. I. Hatfield, Dennis D. II. Title.
  BV652.9.C67   1994
  250—dc20   93-33081
                                                            CIP

94 95 96 97 98 99 00 01 02 03—10 9 8 7 6 5 4 3 2 1

MANUFACTURED IN THE UNITED STATES OF AMERICA

Contents

❖

A Sample Map with Symbols Identified

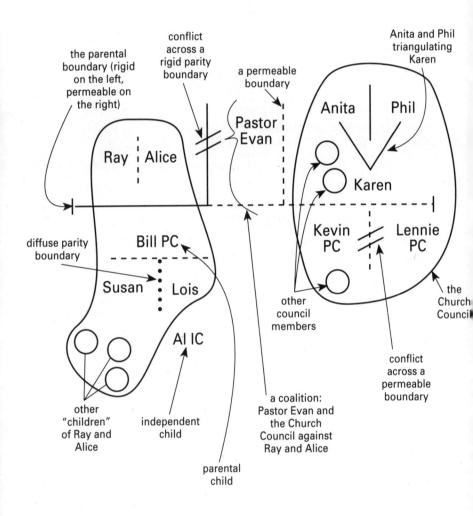

the parental boundary (rigid on the left, permeable on the right)

conflict across a rigid parity boundary

a permeable boundary

Anita and Phil triangulating Karen

Ray ¦ Alice

Pastor Evan

Anita   Phil

Karen

diffuse parity boundary

Bill PC

Kevin PC   Lennie PC

Susan   Lois

the Church Council

other council members

Al IC

other "children" of Ray and Alice

independent child

a coalition: Pastor Evan and the Church Council against Ray and Alice

conflict across a permeable boundary

parental child

Preface

❖

This book is the product of a friendship that goes back to seminary days when we first began reflecting on the "psychology" of a congregation in which we were both serving. We wanted to understand that congregation theologically, spiritually, and psychologically in ways that integrated these three categories.

In 1983, while he was serving as a pastor and working as a certified family therapist in the State of Michigan, it occurred to Dennis that the church he served was not unlike the troubled families he worked with. Thus the idea that led to this book was born, and we have been developing that idea together through work with local church pastors ever since.[1]

The aim of this book is to provide church leaders, and pastors in particular, with a fresh approach to resolving church conflict and helping their congregations toward greater maturity. Our thesis is that behind the official systems of the local church (its offices, boards, committees, etc.) there is another system, a *familylike* system, which powerfully determines the way that church members relate to one another, do business together, care for one another, and fight with one another. Our approach provides a way of discovering this system and working to change it so that the church family is better able to handle its inevitable internal conflicts and becomes a more nurturing system for all its members.

Family systems theory has been around for some forty years, and the effectiveness of family systems therapy is now well documented.[2] It is only recently, however, that family systems theory has been applied to the congregation as a familylike system.[3] Edwin H. Friedman's book, *Generation to Generation*,[4] considers the way in which the family system of the minister interacts with the family system of the congregation, and Kenneth Mitchell's book, *Multiple Staff Ministries*, applies family systems theory to church staff relations.[5] We highly recommend these pioneering works. Our own approach supplements them and introduces a concept of family structure, which we have adapted from the family systems model of Salvador Minuchin.[6]

Most practicing family therapists are eclectic, even if they operate within basically one model. We, too, borrow freely from the work of other family therapists besides Minuchin. We especially value, for example, the work of Virginia Satir,[7] because communication theory is central to our method.[8] But our basic orientation is the structural approach of Minuchin, which we have found to be especially powerful in illuminating congregational dynamics. In adapting Minuchin's theory to the local church, however, we have modified it in significant ways, based on what we have discovered to be the distinctive ways in which the congregation is familylike.

The case studies that inform our work derive exclusively from Protestant churches in North America (Methodist, Baptist, and Presbyterian) and have included both "white" (European American) and "black" (African American) congregations.[9] They have ranged in size from very small (membership less than thirty-five) to mid-size (225-450) congregations, with every size in between.[10] The pastors serving in these churches have included both men and women.

We are especially aware that we have developed our church family concepts to a large extent out of our own

European American Protestant experience. Readers from other traditions and cultural experiences will recognize this at various points. For example, whites and blacks in America tend to use different styles of verbal conflict,[11] and though the pastor is almost always a "parent" figure in the family system of the black church, this is often not the case in white churches.[12]

This book is full of stories. Most are factual (with names and places changed), but some are fictional. (Fictional stories are identified by an invitation to "imagine"—for example, "Let's imagine a church board meeting . . .") Yet we trust that all will ring true for those who have any intimate knowledge of life in the local church. Above all we hope that the stories, theory, and method we provide will help readers discover their own church family system and utilize the insights born of that discovery for more effective ministry in the household of God.

Charles H. Cosgrove
Dennis D. Hatfield

The only sociological category that could possibly be compared to the church, and even then only approximately, is . . . the family.

—Dietrich Bonhoeffer

Chapter One

❖

We're Building You a House

Mark and Sue Rivers took turns tickling Micah, who lay between them on his back, curling his two-year-old body in spasms of laughter on the big white bedspread. Micah stopped to breathe between giggles, and in the silence, which lasted just a moment, a noise came from downstairs. A door had opened and closed. Someone was in the house.

Mark Rivers was a twenty-four-year-old seminary student and pastor of Oakridge Presbyterian Church, a small rural congregation that had been drawing its ministers from a not-too-distant seminary for the past fifteen years. Pastorates at Oakridge tended to be short, most lasting not longer than a year or two. Student pastors said they found ministry at Oakridge extremely frustrating and usually emotionally painful for themselves and their families. None stayed on after graduation. Oakridge wanted to change that pattern with Mark, who happened to be the youngest student pastor they had ever employed.

After Mark had been there a year, they built a parsonage, so that instead of commuting from the seminary on week-ends he could live near the church and take on more pastoral responsibilities. Mark lightened his seminary course load and became a full-time pastor, assuming that with this increase in responsibility he would acquire more authority. He was disappointed.

The church leadership never seemed to take his ideas seriously or to involve him genuinely in decision making. As he saw it, they expected him to "pray, preach, and do visitation" but not to "lead." Eight months later he resigned, saying privately that the experience of pastoring Oakridge had become psychologically unbearable for him and his family. But in the meantime the church had finished the parsonage.

While the parsonage was under construction, Steve Fender, clerk of the session, and Arnie Shanks, one of the elders, would tell Mark and Sue, "We're building you a house." In fact, Arnie was doing some of the carpentry work, and other members of the congregation were engaged in the construction work, too. Mark and Sue resented the contention that the church was building a house for them, pointing out repeatedly that the house was to be a parsonage owned by the church.

The claim, "We're building you a house," seemed especially hollow when Al, an elder, informed them of a plan to design a large room in the basement to serve as both a family room and a church meeting room. He explained that this arrangement would save on heating costs in winter. Mid-week church meetings could be held in the parsonage, so it wouldn't be necessary to heat the church building during the week.

There was only one entrance to the house, which meant that people attending a church meeting in the basement room would pass through Mark and Sue's living quarters.

Mark insisted that any church meetings in his family room would have to be by invitation from him and his wife. Church leaders did not seem to understand his concern.

When the parsonage was nearly finished, Mark and his family moved in. It was only a week later that they heard the noise downstairs. Mark met Arnie in the kitchen. Arnie had come to retrieve some of his tools and had let himself in without knocking. Mark was furious and tried to tell Arnie so, but he had difficulty in adequately explaining his feelings.

Mark told his friend Frank about what had happened. Frank shook his head in wonder. After they'd talked awhile, Frank exclaimed, "Sounds as if the church leaders are treating you like a foster child."

"What do you mean?" Mark asked, his eyes widening.

"Well," Frank said, "they give you a room in their house, but it's clear all along that it's not really your room. You get the message over and over that you are not really one of the adults and that you are only a temporary member of the family—really an outsider. The bounds of your privacy are not respected, almost as if you were a mistreated foster child. And that seems to be how you feel."

"There are at least four couples in the church who are foster parents," Mark said. "And I'm talking about a church that only has about ten core families. One of the foster parents is Steve, clerk of the session. He's been charged with abuse of one of his foster children. Another foster parent is one of the elders, and he also has been charged with abuse of a foster child."

This story is not fictional. If it sounds unlikely, that is probably because we are not accustomed to thinking about the church in the categories of real family life. Although we often speak of the church as a family, even "God's family," we are not predisposed to applying family metaphors realistically to the church. The purpose of this book is to change the way we think about the church as God's family and to provide guidance for helping conflict-ridden church families to heal and mature.

The Familylike Nature of the Local Church

The family is the most basic source of social behavior. Our "families of origin" (the families we grow up in) establish patterns of social behavior in us that we go on to replicate in the larger world, including the world of the congregation. "Put together all the current existing families," says family therapist Virginia Satir, "and you have society." As she sees it, "Institutions such as schools, churches, businesses, and government are, by and large, extensions of family forms to non-family forms."[1]

The family form can be described further if "the role of follower is the role of child."[2] That makes the role of leader like the role of a parent. Since all organized groups have leaders and followers, they all imitate the family form in one way or another.

As leaders and followers in the church family, people replicate family patterns that they learned while growing up. But present or concurrent family systems also influence how they relate to one another in the congregational family. At Oakridge Presbyterian Church, influential church leaders, who were also allegedly abusive foster parents, treated pastors like foster children. And the rest of the church joined in. The problems plaguing Mark Rivers' relationship with the church were in large measure systemic and familial.

If you asked Bill Lewis to describe what it means to be part of Belleville Baptist Church, he'd probably say something like, "We're just one big happy family." If you asked the same question of Bill's pastor, Steve Adams, he might say, "This place is a zoo." And if you asked Bill's wife, Phyllis, she'd shrug her shoulders and maybe make a snide remark.

Suppose you asked the apostle Paul to describe the church at Galatia. Would he call it "one big happy family"? He does urge the Galatians to "do good to all and especially to members of the family of faith" (Gal. 6:10). But in another place he says, "If you bite and devour one another, take care that you don't consume each other!" Perhaps the Galatians are one big fighting family.

Then there is the church at Corinth. Paul uses familial language to describe the Corinthian Christians. He also calls them "babies" (1 Cor. 3:1).

Somewhere between the positive ideal of the church as God's family and the social reality of the way people relate to one another in the church there lies the social fact of the church as God's family.[3] The church *is* the family of God, with all the different happy and unhappy forms of family life that human beings are able to invent for themselves. In fact, in a certain respect the church can be regarded as a family apart from its identity as God's family. As a social organization the church is already familylike. In order to explain more fully what this means, we will examine some biblical teachings about the church as a "family."

The Familylike Nature of the Early Church

New Testament scholars have compared the churches founded by Paul with other types of social organization in the Greco-Roman world in order to discover what models of organization may have influenced the early Christians when they formed their associations with one another. For our interests it is especially significant to discover that the household was "the basic context within which most if not all the local Pauline groups established themselves."[4]

The beginning of the church in "households" probably means that before there was any theological understanding of the church as "God's family," the first believers were already organizing themselves in family settings and along familylike lines. Before Paul called the church God's household, the church was already a kind of household meeting in homes. Early Christians met in private homes and named themselves according to these meeting-places ("the church in the house of—").[5] They started applying kinship language to one another: brother, sister, mother, father. Once the early churches had established themselves in these ways as "families," preachers and teachers like Paul began to declare that they were God's family, God's "household."[6] These early theologians claimed the family metaphor for spiritual use.

Paul, more than any other New Testament writer, applies family terminology to the church. He addresses believers with the familial titles "brother(s)," "sister(s)," and "child(ren)." In several instances he styles himself a "father" to his churches and includes other Christian leaders within the same description (1 Cor. 4:15; 1 Thess. 2:11; Philem. 10). On one occasion he uses maternal imagery to describe his apostolic work of bringing churches into being (Gal. 4:19). He tells the Corinthians that they have "many pedagogues but not many fathers" (1 Cor. 4:15), thus applying to some of their leaders the title of a household servant (the *paidagōgos*) who was entrusted with a parental role of supervision. At the same time he suggests that persons like himself have been parents to the community in a fuller and perhaps more authentic sense. To the Thessalonians he says he has been "gentle as a nurse" (1 Thess. 2:7), and so compares himself with another type of household servant (the *trophos*), one charged with the parental role of caring for and nurturing children.

In 1 Corinthians 3, Paul describes how he had spoken to the Corinthians as "infants in Christ" because they were not spiritually mature, a condition evident in the fact that they squabbled like children (vv. 1-3). But Paul does not always use the metaphor of child negatively. In Philemon, for example, he uses the phrase "my child" positively of Onesimus (v. 10), the slave of Philemon who became a Christian under Paul's influence. Another positive use is found in 1 Corinthians 4:14. "I do not write these things to shame you," Paul explains, "but to admonish you as my beloved children." It may be that 1 Thessalonians 2:7 contains a mixed metaphor: "We were babes among you, like a nurse caring for her children." In 1 Corinthians 14:20, Paul uses the verb *nēpiazein* (related to *nēpios*, "babe") in a positive sense: "Brothers and sisters, do not be children in your thinking; rather, be infants in evil, but in thinking be adults" (NRSV).

We can distinguish between two uses of familial language in Paul. There is first of all the parental relationship established by Paul's apostolic begetting of children through his evangelistic missionary work. As he puts it in 1 Corinthians 4:15, "I begat you in Jesus Christ through the gospel." The same idea is found in Philemon 10 and Galatians 4:19. On the basis of this apostolic parenthood, Paul assumes authority over his churches. The apostle is like a father in a Greco-Roman family, who exercises authority over his children. The clearest expression of this is found in 1 Corinthians 4:14-21, from which we have already cited several sentences.

The second familial pattern suggested by Paul's use of kinship language is the parental relation of God to believers, established by the Spirit. The Spirit adopts believers into Jesus Christ, the offspring of God, in whom they become children of God and thus constitute the "family of faith" (Gal. 6:10; cf. 1 Tim. 3:5). As a result of adoption by the Spirit into God's family, existing kinship relations become a basis for new kinships. Accordingly, Paul addresses Apphia (Philemon's wife?) as "our sister" (Philem. 2) and greets the mother of a certain Rufus as "a mother to me also" (Rom. 16:13).

Not everything that Paul says can be applied directly to contemporary congregations. Paul's own cultural assumptions are embedded in his language. One especially evident cultural feature is his language of "hierarchy." But, as we shall also see, Paul challenges his culture even on this point, which was taken so much for granted by people in his day.

Paul lived in a culture that was strongly patriarchal. The male head of the household was regarded as the supreme authority in the house. As a rule, property was passed on to the sons. If other members of the household (his wife, slaves, children) wished to participate in power, typically they could only do so by influencing him. Society did not give servants and women anything approaching equal authority with men.

Paul challenges the traditional hierarchy of patriarchy in three ways. First, he establishes that the Spirit gives people their ministries in the church, including leadership ministries. The Spirit does so "as it wills" (1 Cor. 12:11). If a woman in one of Paul's churches seeks to exercise leadership (as a prophet or apostle, for example), any who object must take up their objection with the Spirit. Appeals to tradition, the law, custom, "what everybody knows," or to any other accepted norm that excludes women from positions of authority are not valid objections. For the Spirit is forming a new creation, not enforcing what may or may not be valid rules for the old creation.

Second, Paul affirms explicitly that in Christ "there is neither Jew nor Greek, slave nor free, male nor female" (Gal. 3:28). Being a "Greek" (a "Gentile") or an indentured servant does not disqualify one from leadership in the church of the new creation. Nor does being a woman.

Third, Paul himself recognizes women as co-leaders with him in ministry and as leaders in the churches he has founded. Two notable examples are Junia, whom Paul calls an apostle in Romans 16:7, and Phoebe, whom he refers to in Romans 16:1-2 as a "deacon" (meaning "minister") and a "benefactor" (meaning that he depended on her for financial support). This practice of recognizing the co-authority of women with men in the church speaks volumes about Paul's basic Christian convictions. It shows how he himself interprets both the Spirit's work of new creation and the new creation "rule" that he lays down in Galatians 3:28.

It is true that in some places Paul seems to hedge his radically egalitarian views or even flatly to contradict them. But we think that Paul does clearly establish that the Spirit makes people leaders in the church without consideration of sex, class, caste, or ethnic identity. The Spirit of God is "no respecter of persons." And it is this principle that we adopt in defining God's vision for the church as "family" today.

A Family Systems Approach to Church Conflicts

The early church became familylike in a social sense before it began to think of itself as God's family. This means that we today can apply the metaphor of "family" to the early church in two different—but ultimately related—senses. We can say that as a social organization the early churches of Paul's mission were "familylike." We can also say that as spiritual creations these churches were "households of God." Then we can bring these two meanings of the familial metaphor together: by understanding the spiritual identity of the church as a divine summons to the church to become socially a familylike organization. In making the congregation a spiritual family, the Spirit calls it to reform its natural family life in accord with the new humanity in Christ.

This call challenges the familylike social patterns of the local congregation with a vision of the new creation in Christ. If the familylike structure of a local congregation tends to grant authority primarily or exclusively to men, the call to be God's family is a challenge to become a community in which women and men are equal partners in leadership. If the style of authority in a local congregation is paternalistic, the call to be God's family is a challenge to learn a nurturing style of authority. Various patterns of church family authority are described more fully in chapter 3.

How Family Systems Theory Helps

Using a systems approach, we wish to help church leaders deal with church family conflict in a way that furthers the journey of the church toward becoming the family God intends it to be. To do that we begin by using family systems theory to clarify the social ways in which congregations are familylike.

Family systems theory originated during the 1950s, when psychotherapists working in marriage counseling, child guidance, and the treatment of schizophrenia began thinking about the psychological problems of individuals in systemic terms.[7] Instead of assuming that the causes of a particular psychological problem are to be found primarily in the individual psyche, psychotherapists began asking whether the causes may not lie in the relational patterns that exist among family members over time.

From here it was only a short step to viewing any person brought by a family to a therapist as merely the identified patient. The identified patient is the one that the family claims is sick, when in reality the family as a whole needs care. So family therapists began treating whole families as patients.

The local church is a large familylike system made up of many smaller familylike subsystems. It is often the scene of fights, and in almost every congregation the pastor can name those "problem people" or "troublemakers" who seem to create all the conflicts: persons with overt and covert behavior that continually produces crises which interrupt or block ministry and injure the life of the church family. One hopes, secretly or openly: If only they would leave, then we could finally get on with ministry. But either the troublemakers don't leave or, if they do, they are replaced by others.

Conflict is normal in family life, and the emotions that go with it (anger, frustration, exasperation) are also normal. It is impossible to give a simple definition of conflict, except to say that it is the expression (in words and actions) of disharmony between different opinions and desires present in all human systems. Conflict is sometimes overt, taking the form of an argument or even a "church fight." But often it remains hidden, manifesting itself in seemingly trivial ways, as we shall see. And sometimes a seemingly petty open quarrel is really only a mask for a deeper and more serious quarrel beneath the surface.

Conflict is normal in family life, but the repetition of the same conflict (or the same sorts of conflicts) over and over without resolution suggests a problem in the congregational family—a problem that can be treated only if the system is treated as a whole. A systems approach means viewing so-called problem people as likely signs of wider unhealth in the church family. It asks what there is about the congregational family system that encourages and sustains the problem person's objectionable behavior, whatever it may be.

In advocating a systems approach to pastoral care, we are simply applying to the local church the now widely held dictum that individuals don't change unless change happens in the systems in which they live. This generalization is a crucial insight of social psychology and one that deserves to be kept in tension with the premise of individualism: that individuals can also go against the grain of the worlds in which they live.

We esteem pastoral counseling and know the importance of discerning when persons ought to be referred to professional psychotherapists. We also accept individualism as a limited truth. Our aim is to balance this truth with the insight that individuals are profoundly influenced by the systems in which they live. This requires supplementing the traditional counseling ministry with one that attends to the structural and systemic dimensions of congregational life.

Over the past forty years the modern pastoral care movement has encouraged us to practice pastoral care primarily in a counseling mode. When pastors confront so-called problem people, the traditional model of pastoral care encourages them to minister to these persons primarily through counseling (or referral, if that is indicated). Pastors who have faith in the effectiveness of individual psychotherapy, supplemented in some cases by family therapy, imagine that if destructive people receive the counseling they need, they will quit making trouble in the church. Pastors who are skeptical or cynical about the effectiveness of solving church conflicts through counseling may resort to political strategies designed to exclude such persons from power. Or they may turn to methods gleaned from the growing literature on conflict management.

We value the insights and techniques that the more recent conflict management field has brought to pastoral leadership. Our approach offers its own strategies for dealing with church conflicts, but it also provides a framework of interpretation for practicing conflict management techniques more effectively.

Conflict management depends on getting people to voice their real concerns and to act rationally. But as family therapist Edwin Friedman observes, people don't always reveal their real complaints. Often they prefer to mask what's really bothering them by fighting over other issues.[8] One of the greatest advantages of a family systems approach is that it helps identify the issues that are masked by the stated issues.

These hidden issues are typically "familial" in character. For example, congregational criticisms of pastoral functioning may arise when a pastor who is deeply involved with his congregational "family" pulls back emotionally because of changes in his own family life. Criticisms of the pastor's preaching and administration may be only symptomatic of the emotional hurt that members of the congregation are feeling because the pastor no longer seems to be focused emotionally on them.

Kenneth Haugk points out that congregations are favorite arenas for "antagonists," and he suggests that this is because people often assume that antagonists must be placated.[9] There is considerable merit in this explanation. Congregational systems, however, don't merely tolerate antagonists; they *use* them. A congregation will often display ambivalence about the presence of so-called troublemakers, because for all the pain that antagonists cause they may still fulfill some valued function in the system. This is what a systems approach can reveal.

For example, at Sable Valley Community Church, a couple we'll call John and Jane engaged in all sorts of injurious behavior, which qualified them as full-fledged antagonists. (In a later chapter we will examine the role of this couple in the Sable Valley congregational family system.) Without rehearsing all the destructive activities of John and Jane over the course of several years at Sable Valley, we can summarize their behavior by saying that it consisted of brazen lie upon lie and of seemingly cruel indifference to other people's feelings—all of which the couple repeatedly denied with unflinching self-righteousness. Given these facts it may come as a surprise to learn that they were continually reelected to church offices.

Pastor Peter Wells and the deacons eventually began a formal process to deal with John and Jane. The church constitution called for the leadership to follow the familiar guidelines laid down in Matthew 18:15-17, and this they did with great care and patience. But it turned out that John and Jane were themselves very skilled at manipulating the process to their own advantage. The lies and outrages continued. Nevertheless, the deacons were tenacious, and finally, after several months of careful work, they brought a well-founded recommendation to the church that John and Jane's membership be revoked.

The deacons maintained their unanimity throughout the all-church business meeting where the matter was discussed. They supported their case with witnesses, who confronted an unrepentant John and Jane. They also provided other documentation. Peter was certain that the church would vote in favor of the recommendation, because virtually every family in the church had come to him at one time or another to report some injury done to them by John and Jane. But to Peter's surprise, the recommendation did not carry. It wasn't that people thought the recommendation or the process had been unfair to John and Jane. Almost everyone agreed that the deacons had been evenhanded and that they'd been faithful to the church constitution and the Bible.

Later Peter reflected from a family systems point of view on what had happened. He asked himself whether revoking the membership of John and Jane would have violated some unspoken (and therefore unaddressed) church family rule. He also asked whether the church family system had a use for John and Jane's behavior. Did John and Jane serve a purpose in the family system that no one was prepared to name? Considered in this light, it appeared that there were, in effect, certain unspoken agreements between the couple and the church, agreements that prevented church members from doing what they all said—some in public, almost all in private—would have been the right thing.

Nurturing the Church Family System

The church family structure is often more powerful than the official church structure embodied in offices and boards. A congregational family systems model provides a means of discovering this informal family structure behind the official structure. The method based on this model provides strategies for translating that understanding into pastoral action to deal with conflict, open up chronic blockages to ministry, and help the church to become a more nurturing family. These strategies are a combination of immediate responses to crises and continuing efforts at restructuring the family system.

In everyday congregational situations the pastor always has two opportunities for ministry: helping to facilitate the activity at hand (whether church work, celebration, or play) and nurturing those engaged in that activity. Without suggesting that one can always see to the business at hand and to the human relationships involved with equal devotion, we are offering a model that locates the care of family members within the process of doing the business. That is, a family systems approach suggests forms of systemic care that do not entail "stopping the business" for the sake of caring for persons. Although it is sometimes right to stop the business in order to give care, the family system itself can be cared for most effectively while it's operating.

In this respect pastors have an advantage over family therapists. The greatest limitation on family therapy is the difficulty of enacting family life in a therapist's office. Pastors belong in a much more natural way to the congregational family system. Pastors do not need to get their congregational families to carry on normal interactions in their presence; they already find themselves in numerous congregational family situations where these interactions continually take place. Whether during a committee meeting, a church potluck, a service project, or any other gathering of the church, the pastor has frequent opportunities for doing family systems work as part of the ordinary continuing activity of congregational family life.

Let's consider one such opportunity. Imagine a meeting of a local church board. Eight persons, including pastor Rhonda Chandler, are seated around a large table. At some point in the meeting, Carl Graves, the chair of the board, brings up a problem about some unauthorized purchases. According to Henry Lewis, who is also seated at the table, the purchases were made by Alan Fletcher, who is not a board member and therefore is not present.

Carl: . . . I'm not going to see Alan Fletcher get away with this sort of thing again.

Pastor Rhonda: Henry, what is it about these purchases?

Henry: I guess Alan thought they were necessary for remodeling the junior department Sunday school room. He told me—

Carl: He claims we authorized the purchases and that the trustees O.K.'d them.

Rhonda: Let me hear from Henry, Carl. Go ahead, Henry.

Henry: He said that we authorized the purchases when we O.K.'d the ones from a month ago.

Carl: Jerry and Art and I want this business stopped. We want to bring Fletcher before this board and have him give an account to us of all the purchases and we'll see who authorized what.

Rhonda: Did you want to say something, Jerry?

Jerry: No, like Carl said, whatever's the right thing to do.

Rhonda: Well, Carl just said that you are advocating something very specific, having Alan come before us and give us a direct accounting. Is that your feeling?

Jerry: I'm not exactly there. I think, like Carl said, we've got to do something.

Rhonda: I think you're right about that. What about you, Art? Where are you on this?

Art: I think we need to do something—think about what we ought to do. But, you know, Alan's not here to explain himself, so maybe we shouldn't jump to conclusions.

Carl: O.K., but it's not like this is the first time. We can't just keep letting Alan Fletcher pull these stunts.

Rhonda: (*smiling*) This is one of the things I really like about you, Carl. You say exactly what you think about something without dancing around the issue. So, O.K. Carl, who has the bill? Has it been paid?

Carl: I think Phyllis, and I don't know if she's paid it. I told her not to pay on it just yet.

Rhonda: O.K. So Carl, why don't you and I check out the facts—talk to Alan, Phyllis, and Bob (*chair of the trustees*). Then we can bring a recommendation back to the board, if that's appropriate.

What has Rhonda been doing in this meeting, besides helping to deal with the question of an alleged unauthorized expenditure? She has been enforcing and modeling rules of good communication in order to modify the relationships of the people around the table. Carl has made himself the spokesman for Jerry and Henry. He talks for them, and they allow him to do so, even when what he says doesn't represent their views. So, while the pastor is seeking to contribute to a fair handling of the issue that Carl has introduced, she is also working on restructuring the relationships between Carl, Jerry, and Henry and the rest of the members of the board. While she is working on the church business, she is also nurturing the church family.

Rhonda's nurture, practiced consistently with this board over time, will affect the wider congregational family as well. A change in one part of a system always evokes some adjustment by the rest of the system.

Rhonda is in fact doing just the sort of thing in the deacon board meeting (which is a congregational "subsystem") that family therapist Salvador Minuchin does in his work with troubled families. While the family in a therapy session is focused on an issue—such as a child who has been starting fires—Minuchin himself focuses on family structure. While the church board is focused on an issue—such as "another problem with Alan Fletcher"—Rhonda focuses on the group's informal structure, the hidden system that governs how it handles issues. Minuchin suspects that the child's fire-starting is related to something in the family structure. Pastor Rhonda suspects that there may be a connection between the case of the unauthorized expenditure by a so-called problem person and some structural aspects of the church family system. And she is convinced that the "problem" of Alan Fletcher is not going to go away if she focuses only on him as the troublemaker. She must think systemically.

Learning New Terms

This book examines the informal congregational system and its familylike structure. In using the metaphor of "family" to interpret the congregational system, we will be speaking of "parents," "parental children," and "children." We cannot stress too frequently that we are using these categories metaphorically and not literally. Further still, we are not using these familial metaphors to describe people's emotional maturity. The terms *parent* and *child* refer to positions of authority in the informal family system. We are suggesting that congregations structure themselves informally in familylike patterns, where some members are like "parents" and others like "children."

We will define more precisely what we mean by these metaphors in the chapters to follow. Here it is enough to say that the parental metaphor refers primarily to informal authority in the church, apart from the authority that inheres in offices, boards, committees, and so forth (the official structures). When we apply the metaphors of parent and parental child to specific people, this does not in itself mean that they are good parents. It only means that they have a parentlike role for other members in the congregation. It is also important to emphasize at the outset that our use of the family metaphor does not mean we support all the ways in which people "idealize" the church as a "family." Often people hold up as a model for the church what is little more than a cultural ideal of "the American family" in some past or present version. Such a church merely imitates the culture instead of challenging cultural values and norms from a Christian perspective.

Without defining family language carefully, one can inadvertently reinforce unhealthy styles of parenting and can trigger painful associations in persons who have suffered emotional or physical abuse by a parent or other family member. Each person brings his or her own definitive experience to what "father," "mother," or "child" means. Hence, it is better to avoid such language altogether than to use it in a naive way on the false assumption that it conveys a single idea to everyone and carries positive and constructive connotations for all.

As we have explained, "the church as family" is in fact a double metaphor. On one hand it describes what the church is called to be: the family of God. But the local congregation is already familylike in a second way. As a social institution it is familylike quite apart from whether it lives up to the image of the new humanity in Christ. We hope that readers will keep clearly in mind this distinction between "is" and "called to be." In the chapters to follow, we will be describing congregational families according to the way they "are" and will be suggesting what they might become in response to God's call. Most important, we will be offering systemic pastoral strategies for helping conflicted church family systems become more like the households of nurture that we believe God calls them to be.

Chapter Two

❖

Church Family Structure

We've already mentioned Steve Adams. He's twenty-eight years old and in the second wearying year of his pastorate at Belleville Baptist Church, a small congregation averaging 85 in attendance at Sunday morning worship. During his two-year tenure the church has grown by 20 percent. But these have not been happy months of ministry for Steve. Week after week he has been confronted with conflicts. One concerned the choir.

As Steve tells the story, it all began when Margaret, a member of both the choir and the music committee, quit the choir. "Then a couple of other people got a hold of me and told me they were going to quit, too, because they're sick of it all." Sick of conflicts in the choir and frustrated with the fact that "we had children coming up into the choir loft during worship service and sitting with their parents, and leaving and going back and forth."

According to Steve, there is no focused leadership in the choir. The "director-organist," Al, doesn't take charge. Instead, Denise (Margaret's best friend) leads rehearsals and selects anthems for worship. At least she does so when she's there, but she isn't always there. When she's absent, Margaret manages things. "Or maybe someone else." There is never any certainty that what the choir practices as its anthem for the upcoming Sunday will in fact be the anthem it sings when Sunday morning arrives.

One week Steve's sister was visiting from out of town. Steve arranged for her to provide special music that Sunday morning. Denise was on vacation, so Steve made the arrangements with Al (the person with the title and salary of "director"). When Sunday morning came, Denise showed up and selected an anthem, only to discover that the pastor had scheduled someone else in place of the choir. She was furious that he had not consulted her. "But you were out of town," Steve explained, thinking to himself "how she's not even the director of the choir, so why should I have to consult her?"

Conflicts like this one frustrated Steve and caused tension in the choir. As Steve saw it, the choir ought to have clear leadership, so that he wouldn't get caught in misunderstandings over whom he should talk to in coordinating plans for worship.

Steve decided to call what he announced as a "reorganizational meeting of the choir." It would take place on a Wednesday night after Bible Study, which was not the regular practice time for the choir. He published the announcement for three consecutive weeks in advance of the meeting. Part of the announcement read: "It's a must that every adult member interested in singing in the choir be there." Later Steve had second thoughts about this statement. "Evidently it was interpreted in a variety of ways." But he had wanted to "get the choir's attention and make sure everyone showed up."

Margaret showed up, despite the fact that she'd quit. Denise didn't come, but her husband Jack did. He's the only man in the choir. Steve began the meeting by speaking about the nature of ministry and the choir members' roles as ministers, emphasizing "a certain responsibility and need for commitment." But Jack kept breaking in, with comments like, "I have something to say about that. . . . They didn't do their part, and, look, if the organist would just have us sing songs weeks in advance . . ." As Steve recalled the meeting, it was full of arguments and disorder:

> [Jack] kept interrupting me before I even got to the actual conflict. I basically said it seems like we have two options with the choir. Either we can disband, because it seems like some people want to quit, and we need people to have a choir. Or we can reorganize and become more disciplined and work on how we function as a choir. From that point on the meeting degenerated. People started making accusations, and I lost total control.

Afterward Jack informed Steve that he and Denise were no longer members of the choir. "And all the members of the choir were saying, 'Well, what can we do to keep you? What can we do to get you back? Oh, we can't have this rift in the choir.' " But Steve was thinking, "Let them go, let them go." He judged that "this would be a step forward," because "it's Jack and Denise who don't want to have practice on Wednesday night because they live a half an hour away." And that's "kind of the incident in a nutshell."

If we were focusing on Steve and his own pastoral style, we might begin to explore why he felt it was necessary that he call such a meeting. Or why he speaks to his church in the language of either-or options and with a strong intimation that they're not measuring up to some unspecified standard of his own. But we assume that a system is at work here, a system in which Steve's pastoral responses are only one element. And because they are part of the system, we cannot explore them as if they represented an independent response, the fruit of Steve's own ministerial training, personality, and theology alone. So we start with the system itself, beginning with the pieces before us. In order to do that we must first gain some understanding of what church family systems look like and how they operate.

The Structure of Authority

The key to understanding the power dynamics at work in church conflict is to grasp the nature of boundaries. Boundaries have two aspects: structure of authority and quality of communication.

In terms of structure, boundaries reflect implicit relations of leadership and deferral operative within the family system. In terms of quality, boundaries within the congregational family are defined by patterns of communication.

Structure refers to divisions that establish "parents" and "children." Quality refers to the degree and clarity of communication across a boundary. Every boundary defines both structure of relationship and quality of communication between the parties who interact "across" it. We will spell out these distinctions with examples in greater detail later.

Structure is also the division of the family into subsystems. Subsystems are groups of persons who are affiliated with one another. Official organization often fosters such affiliations, so that a Sunday school class, a "circle" group, or any of the many fellowship groups that churches establish may become family subsystems. But in many cases it is a prior sense of family kinship that leads people to establish such groups ("The Home Builders," "The Thirties Something," etc.). And sometimes the unspoken family rules for belonging to a subsystem exclude persons who "technically" qualify.

Official groups, such as the church staff and church council (deacon board, session, etc.), also often function simultaneously as official and family subsystems. It is important, however, to keep these two identities distinct. A church board has an official parent function. But its members may not be parents in the unofficial family system. They may be children and "parental children" (defined later) who belong to a family subsystem, beyond the board, that has its own indigenous congregational parents.

It should be clear now that there are many different subsystems in a congregational family. In fact, each person is a subsystem while belonging to other larger subsystems.

To understand church conflict, it is important to identify family subsystems, because they are fundamental units of power in the congregation. In analyzing any conflict we seek to determine how specific subsystems are related to one another. That means discovering what sorts of boundaries lie between different sets of subsystems.

For example, at Parkside Presbyterian Church there are several informal (family) subsystems. Pastor Tony Matera names and diagrams these subsystems and the boundaries between them in figure 1.

We call such a diagram a church family "map," and we will explain mapping in greater detail in chapter 5. The horizontal line running across the middle of the diagram is the parental boundary. All those above this line (including the Connectional Leaders as an entire subsystem) are parents in the Parkside family. Those below are different kinds

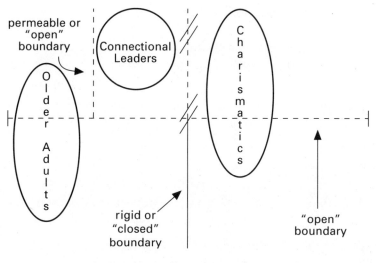

Figure 1

of children. The boundary between the Older Adults and the Charismatics is "closed." The boundaries between the Connectional Leaders and the two other groups are "open." The double slashes across the boundary between the Older Adults and the Charismatics indicate conflict between these two subsystems. There is also conflict between the Connectional Leaders and the Charismatics.

The Quality of Boundaries

When we say that boundaries are "open" or "closed," we are referring to quality of communication. Three basic patterns of communication distinguish boundary quality as porous, rigid, or diffuse. These can be thought of as ranges on a continuum from rigid at one end to diffuse at the other, with the porous boundary lying in the middle. The porous and diffuse boundaries are open. The rigid boundary is closed.

The Porous Boundary (Symbol: - - - - - - - -)

The porous boundary admits communication that is frequent enough and above all clear enough for both sides to understand one another. Sufficient frequency depends on the nature of the relationship and the kinds of interactions that it requires. A frequency rate sufficient to keep a boundary open between two large subsystems in the congregation might not sustain an open boundary between two staff members. But clarity of communication is more important than frequency of interaction. Infrequent interaction between two staff members or two large subsystems may be enough to maintain an open boundary if the quality of communication is clear. In that case we would call the boundary "open."

Imagine a Thanksgiving Day dinner. The extended Walcott family (which also includes Westons, Kohuts, and Pasdros) is gathered at the table.

Vance: What you're saying makes me very angry because you're tearing down an organization that I'm very proud to be a member of.

Larry: I didn't know you were a member of the NRA. I'm sorry. But I still think what I'm saying is right.

Vance: Well, it's people thinking like you do that's the problem with this country.

Leah: Let's not argue. Have some more corn, Vance. Larry, more potatoes?

Vance: I don't want any corn. Listen here. The NRA—

Leah: (rising to go into the kitchen) I'll heat up your plate for you, Vance. Do you want some more turkey?

This interaction between Vance and Larry suggests that the boundary between them is porous.

A porous boundary doesn't mean that the parties involved will always understand one another. It means that they can work through misunderstanding because their pattern of interaction is engaged and each has a clear sense of identity in the relationship.

"Engaged" means a link-up on both sides, not just talking or one-way communication. Though engagement doesn't necessarily reflect emotional involvement between two parties (friendship, affection), it does mean that emotions are being interpreted with some clarity across the boundary.

Where boundaries are porous, people "hear" one another. If two persons sympathize with each other they can do so without confusing the feelings of the other with their own. A porous boundary may be conflicted, but it allows for the conflict to be communicated clearly and openly.

The Rigid Boundary (Symbol: —————)

The rigid boundary admits little genuine communication. It means that the subsystems are not interacting sufficiently and clearly enough for mutual understanding to occur.

Joe, Leah's father-in-law, was also at the dinner table with Larry, Vance, and Leah. Joe listened to Vance and Larry. He didn't pay any attention to Leah. He didn't even notice when she left the table to go into the kitchen or that she stayed there until the argument stopped. He and his daughter-in-law don't argue, but they also don't talk. Joe seems infinitely remote to Leah and it pains her. In fact, she thinks he doesn't like her, and the more silent he grows the more anxious she feels. Joe isn't aware of any of this. The boundary between Leah and Joe is rigid.

A rigid boundary does not necessarily signify conflict, although rigid boundaries are sometimes conflicted. Persons or subsystems whose communication is marked by a rigid boundary will tend to act independently of one another and without an emotional understanding of one another's feelings. This does not mean that there is no feeling connected with the relationship, only that feelings are not being interpreted clearly back and forth across the boundary.

The Diffuse Boundary (Symbol: · · · · · · ·)

The diffuse boundary is a pattern of unclear communication in a specific sense. Enmeshed persons have difficulty distinguishing their feelings from those of the other in the relationship. Unclear communication arises from this diffusion of feelings across the boundary. A diffuse boundary signifies overinvolvement to the point where it is difficult for persons to act independently. Although communication of feelings travels slowly, if at all, across rigid boundaries, emotions echo too quickly through the enmeshed system.

When Vance told Leah, No, I don't want any more corn, Dorothy (Leah's mother) felt upset and couldn't look at Vance. She followed Leah out to the kitchen where they waited until the men's anger toward them subsided.

In fact, the men weren't angry with them, but it felt to Leah and Dorothy like they were. Dorothy didn't even have to mention that she knew just how Leah felt when Vance said he didn't want the corn. They both felt it. It was as if Vance had spoken it to both of them at once. Or so it seemed to them.

Enmeshment is a form of empathy without clear borders differentiating "self" from "others." When two persons are enmeshed with each other, they feel each other's feelings as their own. Those who tend toward enmeshment also feel (or imagine they feel) the emotions of others around them and often confuse these emotions with their own.

It is of the nature of diffuse boundaries that they almost always appear within large subsystems and not between them. They typically form between individuals in pairs or in small groups. By contrast, rigid boundaries occur between subsystems of any size. Rigid boundaries form easily between large subsystems because it is difficult for subsystems composed of large numbers of persons to sustain engagement across a boundary. But rigid boundaries are also common between individuals.

Mixed and Disputed Boundaries

If we think of boundaries as styles of interaction, then we can imagine that in addition to the three simple boundary qualities we have just described there are also hybrids—combinations of boundaries that arise when people with different communication styles and psychological make-ups communicate. In such cases the boundary between them can be described as mixed.

We can symbolize mixed boundaries by drawing two boundary symbols parallel to each other between two subsystems. For example, the boundary between Joe and his wife, Mary Lou, is mixed because Joe has put up a wall, while Mary Lou senses Joe's emotions (or feels that she does). For her it's as if he is radiating feelings that constantly mix with her own emotions, even though he won't talk to her about what he's thinking or feeling. We can symbolize the boundary between them in this way:

$$
\begin{array}{c|c}
 & \bullet \\
 & \bullet \\
 & \bullet \\
\text{Joe} & \bullet \quad \text{Mary Lou} \\
 & \bullet \\
 & \bullet \\
 & \bullet
\end{array}
$$

Mixed boundaries are more apt to take the forms rigid-diffuse or porous-diffuse than rigid-porous. The reason is that the continuing presence of a porous style of communication tends to open up rigid boundaries. It also exerts a clarifying pressure on diffuse boundaries (although diffuse boundaries are harder to change than are most rigid boundaries).[1] The most important thing to note about mixed boundaries is that they don't admit clear and open communication.

But it is not only the basic quality of communication that can differ in the way two parties constitute the boundary between them. Sometimes there are different assumptions about the very nature of the boundary, in which case we refer to the boundary as disputed. A disputed boundary is present in a relationship between two parents in which one regards the other as a child, but the other does not accept that role or defer to the one who projects it on him or her. For example, in a traditionally paternalistic church family, women who do not acquiesce to paternalistic authority and who have their own congregational children often find themselves communicating across disputed boundaries with male parents. We can diagram the disputed boundary by tilting a vertical (parity) boundary to suggest the pressure from one side of the boundary to establish it as a parental (horizontal) boundary:

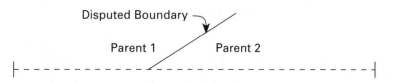

Affiliation Distance Across Boundaries

Any of the three boundaries we have just described can bear an intense or a weak emotional connection or affiliation. As we have already indicated, intense emotional involvement across a rigid boundary does not mean that emotions are being interpreted clearly, only that they are being communicated strongly. We can visualize the degree of affiliation across a boundary as a kind of "space" on either side of the boundary. We refer to this as the affiliation distance across a boundary. A boundary can be open with great distance on either side, meaning little affiliation. It can also be rigid with a high degree of affiliation.

"Loyalty" to another person is an example of affiliation that can take place across any kind of boundary. Strong personal loyalty means that the affiliation distance between persons across the boundary is very narrow, even if the boundary itself is rigid. Affiliation distances are by definition narrow (practically nonexistent) across diffuse boundaries. They may be of any range in the case of porous boundaries.

It is important not to confuse affiliation distance with boundary quality. Close affiliation between people ("They care so much about each other") does not mean that the boundary between them is open or diffuse and cannot be rigid. As we shall see in chapter 3, paternalism in the church family often includes a strong affiliation across a rigid (parental) boundary.

Boundaries and Family Conflict

An understanding of boundaries is critical to dealing with the systems behind church family conflict. Conflict is unavoidable in church families. In this sense it is natural. As all handbooks on conflict management stress, the best way to manage conflict is to treat it as something normal and bring it out into the open where it can be handled fairly and constructively. Fighting openly keeps conflict from festering in insidious ways and gives those involved a chance to deal with it. But conflict is not really out in the open if the fighting is taking place across rigid or diffuse boundaries. It may only seem to be. Where boundaries are rigid or enmeshed, the communication essential to conflict resolution cannot occur, even if the fighting is no longer taking place under the surface.

Conflicts fire across rigid boundaries in escalating volleys that produce increasing distance between the conflicted subsystems. Conflict circulates with greater and greater intensity in enmeshed subsystems, but it is always going nowhere. It cannot be resolved because no one is certain of who feels and thinks what. Sometimes a point of emotional tolerance is exceeded for one of those involved, who reacts in self-defense by erecting a rigid boundary. But that only makes things worse because a rigid boundary is the thing most feared by those who tend toward enmeshment.

If one considers the range of family communication as a continuum from rigid through porous to enmeshed, it is possible to conceive the middle range as wide enough to include porous patterns of engagement that tend toward either enmeshment or rigidity. Neither of these tendencies makes a family dysfunctional. It is the extremes that can injure church family life and ministry. When the system is stressed and conflict erupts, the rigid and enmeshed boundaries in the system stand in the way of conflict resolution. For this reason it is important to work on opening up rigid boundaries and clarifying diffuse ones not only in the midst of a church family conflict but also as a continuing strategy of preparing the system to handle future conflicts more effectively.

Although rigid and diffuse boundaries hinder the family from processing conflict in constructive ways, this does not mean that these types of boundaries are inherently bad. In literal families, maternal care for a newborn often naturally (and healthily) tends toward enmeshment, and there is nothing wrong with an adolescent being disengaged from a much younger sibling.

The same holds for the congregational family. Especially as the congregation grows and becomes more complex, there will be varying styles of interaction between subsystems. Some will be disengaged, others closely knit. A rigid boundary between the Golden Age Circle and the Senior High Youth Group is no cause for concern. Nor is a tendency toward enmeshment between persons who are emotionally close. The test comes when the family undergoes stress. Stress caused by some internal or external change requires, at least for the moment, the exercise of alternative styles of relating. Hence, it is wise for families occasionally to practice alternative styles of interaction. Sometimes one parent can take a vacation from the daily intimate care of an infant and let the other take over. Once in a while, the fifteen-year-old can play a game with the six-year-old. So, too, in the church family. Sometimes the teens and the "Golden Agers" can be involved in an event together, and so forth.

The ideal of "one big happy family" often conjures up a picture of everyone engaged with more or less the same degree of involvement with everyone else. In some people's view, that is what "community" is supposed to mean. But equal engagement between all subsystems is neither practical in a complex family nor necessarily ideal. In a congregation that is middle-sized (100 to 175 average attendance at worship) or larger, the practical ideal is that everyone enjoy continuing and satisfying engagement with some persons, have some regular experiences with the congregation as a whole, and that all subsystems have the capacity to modify their patterns of interaction with one another under stress.

The one necessary qualification to the preceding is that both disengagement and enmeshment as habitual personal styles of interaction are unhealthful. The style of disengagement produces the isolation and alienation of the over-individuated male in American society. The style of enmeshment produces the co-dependence and diffuse self-identity of the underindividuated female in our society. We will say more about this in discussing church family authority in chapter 3.

What Makes a Parent a Parent?

When speaking of the structural aspect of boundaries, Minuchin defines them as "the rules governing who participates and how."[2] Minuchin has literal families in view, in which there is a natural differentiation between parents and children based primarily on social conventions defining the age of adult maturity. This difference creates the most basic boundary in the literal family system: the parental boundary.

At Forest Hill Baptist Church, Earl Camp has taken it upon himself to police the hallways every Sunday morning to make sure that everyone gets to Sunday school class on time. Earl has a little bell that he rings to announce the Sunday school hour. He scolds any children or adults who linger in the hallways or other parts of the building after classes have started.

One Sunday morning Earl came upon a group of young married couples talking among themselves in the church parlor. He reprimanded them for not being in class and told them that they were bad examples to their children. This encounter left two of the young women in tears. One of the couples went home instead of worshiping that morning. The others went to class. Angela Benson (who went to class) later complained about Earl, "He makes me feel like a child." Her husband Rick had the same feeling but didn't say so. He wished he had "told Earl off."

This vignette suggests that in the family system at Forest Hill, Angela and Rick are "children." Earl is a "parent." We would need more information about other interactions to test this tentative judgment. For the sake of illustration, however, we can diagram the family relationships of Angela, Rick, and Earl as follows:

```
                         Earl
|——————————————————————————————————————————|

        Angela               Rick
```

The horizontal line (|-   -|) is a parental boundary. We have indicated its quality as rigid.

The parental boundary refers to the basic division of informal authority in the church family system. In God's household all persons are brothers and sisters as children of God, but in the social family system of any given congregation certain persons will fill parental roles, others child roles.

These roles are not fixed. There is continual movement of children into parental roles, and some persons may operate now in one role, now in another, depending on circumstances. Not only that, each congregation will have its own implicit (and to some extent explicit) understanding of these roles and will operate with its own set of "rules" about who can fill them.

To repeat M. Scott Peck's observation, the role of a follower is the role of a child. Whenever we follow someone else, we assume in some sense a childlike role. And if we usually find ourselves in the role of follower in the congregation, then we are functionally in the role of child in the congregational family.

Although few adults like being labeled "child," many in fact prefer this congregational role for themselves. They would rather make their contribution without the responsibility of leadership. Still others seek leadership responsibility only so long as there is someone else cuing them—some other parent who makes them feel secure. And there are others who aspire to be parents and have the leadership qualities or potential to be good parents in the church family, but they are denied the opportunity by the rules that govern who gets to be a parent in the system.

In our descriptions of particular congregational families, we use the label "parent" to describe actual function and not aspiration or qualification.

The terms *parent* and *child* designate patterns of leadership and deferral. They do not imply value judgments about emotional maturity. To be a child does not mean one is "childish." For example, Rick's restraint in not "telling Earl off " suggests emotional maturity, while one could easily interpret Earl's behavior with the bell as childish. Children may be mature members of the family and may suffer under the childishness of immature congregational parents.

Nor do the metaphors of parent and child refer to a division between those who have power and those who do not. An immature and manipulative congregational child may exercise more power in the system than anyone else. Likewise, manipulative congregational parents possess power beyond their parental power. (We will explain why as we go along.)

The difference between congregational parents and children is solely a matter of authority: recognized power. Those who are acknowledged in the system as having legitimate power, outside of any office they may hold, possess the authority of parents. Parents are those to whom others give deference.

It is important to emphasize that we are using the term *deference* in a technical sense to mean acquiescence to authority. On a given occasion a parent may "give in" to a child or to another parent for any number of reasons. Parents compromise. Parents show patience. Parents choose moments to intervene. Parents may be strict or permissive. But none of these in itself constitutes deference, so long as it is undertaken as a parental choice and not an abdication of the parental role.

But who get to be the parents?

One can find the attitude among some clergy that so-called laypeople are to be viewed with condescension. The pastoral staff may regard themselves in their professional competencies as parents and take pleasure in thinking of the members of the congregation as "children" to be cared for and controlled. Such attitudes, where they are found, are often mythical projections of how some clergy would like things to be. In fact, clergy do not determine who the parents are in the local congregation. The people themselves do. Not only that, pastors cannot become parents in the congregational family system unless the people acknowledge them as parents. And that doesn't happen automatically.

Although it is illuminating to look upon church offices as parental functions within the official church system, it is very important not to confuse these functions with the informal family system. Being a pastor or a member of the governing church board doesn't in itself make one a parent in the congregational family. Consider Belleville Baptist, for example. It turns out that a significant portion of the 20 percent growth in church membership during Steve Adams' ministry at Belleville has come from returnees who left the church when it split twenty years ago. Laverne is one of these. She is now the church clerk and sings in the choir. She's also one of the choir members who told the pastor that the choir was getting so bad that she felt she wanted to quit. So not all the newcomers are new to the congregation. There are also "new oldcomers" among the newcomers. The congregation is giving the new oldcomers and some of the other newcomers positions of leadership. Are any of them congregational parents? One might assume so, but to do so would be to confuse holding an office with being a parent.

From what Steve says, the newcomers, too, remain passive along with everyone else during worship, while literal children wander about virtually at will. Is this because the newcomers share the unspoken family rules that sanction such behavior? Or would they like to change things but enjoy no parental authority to do so? Laverne, for example, remains a spectator during the conflict at the special meeting. Steve says that the other newcomers are frustrated with the choir, but they evidently have no more power than Steve to do anything about it. They seem to accept the rules of the congregation and to tolerate frustration without asserting leadership. If they're bothered by something, they may tell the pastor. But, according to Steve, there is no real conflict between them and the rest of the congregation.

Parents have unofficial authority in the congregational system. At the level of unofficial authority, it is to a significant degree ability that constitutes authority. This is in part what makes a parent a parent.

By ability we don't mean "expert authority." The term *expert* suggests recognized competence in a particular area of knowledge. Nor do we mean skill, unless that term is taken very generally. We have in mind something at once much broader and more focused than expertise or skill, namely, the sort of ability in relating to others that makes some persons leaders and others followers.

Ability to lead may be skillful, but it can also be clumsy. Leaders may wield power without any controlled and calculated strategy of influence (for good or ill). And they may not possess enough mature self-control, including enough independence from their followers, to lead in ways that coincide with their own ultimate goals and values.

Along with ability to lead there is a complementary element that constitutes the functional authority of a congregational parent, namely, that the parent is one who receives deference from others. Followers make leaders out of people who possess the ability and willingness to lead. And they do so by deferring to them. With respect to the congregational family, this means that "the children," through deference, make the parents.

Deference arises not simply through recognition of someone's ability to lead. It also stems from the perceived nature of the relationship between the one who defers and the one who leads. Younger persons are disposed to defer to older ones in the congregation because age has conventionally

been one defining characteristic of familial authority structures. The personal qualities and relational style that we
associate with our own literal parents may lead us to defer
to persons in the congregation who exhibit some of those
same qualities and a similar style. An older man who talks
to Angela the way Earl does when he scolds her makes
Angela feel like a child. Out of that identity she defers to
Earl and thus contributes to his parental authority. But she
does the same thing with certain other parental figures in
the congregation, most of whom treat her kindly. Her
deference toward them, together with the deference they
receive from others, is in part what establishes and sustains
their parental roles.

When those who receive deference from others respond
as "parents," they become parents. Family authority emerges
out of the subtle everyday negotiations by which parents
and children make one another.

Let's look more closely at Belleville Baptist Church to see if
we can discover who the parents and children are. When we
examined the roles of the newcomers in the congregation, we
didn't find evidence to suggest that any of them are serving in
parental roles. Though the church is electing them to offices,
that in itself does not make them parents.

Is Margaret a parent? Pastor Steve Adams doesn't think
so, and we judge that he's probably right. With Steve
present, but not in control of the meeting, Margaret didn't
assert parental leadership. She is also the youngest person
in the congregation.

Steve seems to think that the only person in the choir
who acts like an adult is Laverne. But she is not a recognized
parent in the choir. She ends up on the sidelines, along with

Steve, refusing to participate in the "emotional uproar," as Steve calls it.

Denise stayed home in protest, sending her husband to speak for her. She also exercises leadership in the choir by sometimes choosing music. Then again, so does Margaret, or someone else if neither one of them is present. Evidently the choir listens to Denise when she's around. Lacking additional information, we locate her for the time being above the parental boundary.

When we ask Steve who the most powerful people are in the church, he says he doesn't know. "Nobody comes to mind." He goes on to explain that it's "very diffused" and says "everybody's passive." "I know they have power, but I can't figure out who's got it and who's using it." When we rephrase our question and ask who is the most respected person, Steve answers without hesitation: Bill.

Bill Lewis, born to charter members of the church, has been part of Belleville his whole life. Steve informs us that Bill and his family "have a lot of problems." Bill's wife has been hospitalized on several occasions after "nervous break-downs," and she regularly takes antipsychotic drugs. She has accused Bill of violence toward her. Steve has been uncertain how to intervene.

But "everybody loves Bill." He's a "very slick person," Steve says. What Steve means by slick is that Bill manages to get his way with the congregation. For example, one Wednesday night Steve was ill and couldn't attend the Wednesday evening meeting at church. His wife, Anne, went to the service to deliver the message that the people should have a time of prayer, sing some songs, and go home. There would be no Bible Study because Steve was sick. Anne went over early and found Bill there. (Bill always gets to church events an hour early.) When he found out Steve would be absent, he hurried back home to get some tape recordings of fundamentalist radio debates. That night he had everyone listen to his tapes, which went on for an hour and a half before Anne finally left. "That was typical of Bill," Steve says.

It turns out that Bill also attends all the choir practices, even though he's not in the choir. "And he goes visiting with me, too." That was his job when Steve came. "He tags along with me, but I've learned that important visits I do secretly, without him knowing." The reason is that Bill embarrassed the pastor on a visit to Bill's own daughter and her boyfriend. Neither Bill's daughter Susan nor her boyfriend is involved in the church. During the visit, Steve explains, "Bill started asking her all these questions, like 'You're saved, aren't you? You've made a decision for Christ, haven't you?' Very inappropriate discussions . . ."

Our conversation with Steve about this event continued as follows:

Cosgrove: He asks these questions to his daughter?

Steve: His daughter. Forcing her to talk out in the—I don't know what the need for him to do that was. And it was obvious her boyfriend wasn't very excited about the fact that the preacher and a deacon are there. Bill is also a deacon. (*pause*) Finally . . .

Hatfield: That a preacher and her father were there. (*laughter*)

Steve: (*smiling*) Well, yeah, that's right. It's hard to keep it all straight. I had no intention of doing anything religious at that encounter. Bill grabs his daughter's hand and her boyfriend's hand and says, "Preacher, will you have a word of prayer?" It was a totally inappropriate thing to do. I could tell that the poor guy, her boyfriend, was just a nervous wreck, didn't know what was going on, why this was happening.

Cosgrove: So how about you in that situation?

Steve: I lost—I was out of con—I had—I went ahead and said a very short prayer, "Thank you for your love, God." You know, I mean, just because—if I would have refused to do the prayer in front of, in that situation, that would have created another mess that I just didn't have the energy or the desire to deal with at that time.

Cosgrove: Yeah.

Steve: So afterwards I told Bill, I said, "Bill, why don't you let me decide when I want to pray." I said, "In some situations I don't think it's appropriate to do that." And he said, "Oh! O.K., O.K., O.K." But he's very—he doesn't have any sense of what's socially appropriate. . . . But he's the one who everyone defers to for everything.

Because Steve did not have much respect for Bill and thought of him at best as a harmless nuisance, at worst as an undersocialized person given to violence in the home, it never occurred to him to think of Bill as a congregational parent. But Bill is a parent, perhaps the primary parent, in the Belleville church family. That becomes clear as we ask Steve for more stories about Bill. Immediately Steve remembers, "Well, Bill was involved in the whole thing with the choir."

Hatfield: Oh?

Steve: Yeah, I hadn't thought to mention this, but he was. There's this man, Kurt. He comes to church maybe twice a year. He lives in Florida but comes up to visit. He used to be in the church, I guess. He's got some—he's mentally disabled, I think, in some way. The first time I ever met him—this was a couple of months ago—he came and Bill—this was five minutes before worship service—Bill brought him back and said, "Here, sing in the choir." And the choir members got terribly upset. The guy was just totally disoriented. Here's Bill just bringing him back to sing in the choir. Bill quickly left and the man said, "What do I do? What do I do?" And I said, "Tell you what, you don't need to sing in the choir. Why don't you just go sit in the congregation and join the worship service. Don't feel like you have to sing in the choir." But he went ahead and did anyway because I think he felt forced to by Bill, and he was in an awkward situation. And he didn't have the ability to sort that out in five minutes. The choir—that frustrated, especially frustrated Laverne.

Hatfield: O.K., but how about—

Steve: And Margaret got upset by it.

Hatfield: What upset Margaret about that?

Steve: That he—I guess because it didn't go through her. That was the day she quit the choir, as a matter of fact. After that incident she quit.

Hatfield: Because Bill—

Steve: She blames that incident.

Hatfield: How does she blame? What's her language? What does she say about it?

Steve: At the choir meeting she just said that the day she quit was "the day a certain man"—that's how she talks about it—"the day a certain man came to sing in the choir who had never sung in the choir before," and that just topped it off. "Because," she said, "here he was in the choir, and he didn't know what we were doing, and he didn't know what we were singing, and I was having to explain everything to him." And she said, "It embarrassed me, and I couldn't take it anymore." That's sort of what she said.

Bill is one of the parents at Belleville. When we say this, it's important to understand that we are not evaluating his skill as a parent. We are not suggesting that he is a good parent. What makes Bill a parent is that people in the church defer to him. Even when they don't like what he does or demands, they accede to him. The pastor doesn't have this level of authority. Even Kurt, dragged into the choir by Bill, stays there because Bill put him there. And he remains there even after the pastor has given him permission to leave.

The Independent Child

What distinguishes a parent from a child is the functional exercise of care and leadership by the parent and deference by the child. Therefore no parents can emerge without children. This means that all adults without metaphorical children in the congregation are by definition below the parental boundary.

But there is such a thing as the child without congregational parents, whom we refer to as the independent child.

The independent child has no metaphorical children and is therefore situated below the parental boundary. But the independent child also does not defer to others in forming judgments and opinions. Independent children make up their own minds but have no followers. Laverne, the choir member who stood on the sidelines with Steve during the emotional uproar at the choir meeting, is probably an independent child in the Belleville system.

Independent children are typically the people whom we would characterize as mature adults but who we recognize do not fill parental roles in the congregational family system. Some of them go on to become parents, but others prefer the role of independent child.

Because they make up their own minds, the perspectives of mature independent children can be valuable to any decision-making process; hence, congregational parents should be nurtured to listen to them. It is one of the unhappy facts of church life that so often immature and unskilled parents wield authority in the church family while wise and gifted independent children get pushed to the margins or are labeled troublemakers because they don't unquestioningly accept the status quo.

The Parental Child

We have identified the principal division in the congregation as the parental boundary and have defined parents, children, and independent children. Now we introduce another category of children: the "parental child."

In the literal family, a parental child is an older sibling to whom the parents delegate authority for the care of younger children.[3] But in the church family, parental children are distinguished not by their age or even by being allocated authority from the parents in the system. They acquire their authority in the same way parents do—from congregational children who defer to them.

What distinguishes parental children is the fact that they defer to certain persons (congregational parents) but exercise leadership and care toward other family members (other congregational children). They take their cues from other parental figures and typically defer to these persons when family decisions are made. Once parental children begin to function independently, they become full-fledged parents.

Ellis and Harriet

Jim Roper began having conflicts with Ellis Campbell soon after assuming the pastorate of Evergreen Community Church. Ellis was a seventy-five-year-old retired business-man who liked to keep everybody happy. Jim's preaching rankled Ellis. What Jim thought of as "prophetic" preach-ing, Ellis regarded as "too negative," and he continually chided Jim for it.

Ellis had a close friend named Harriet Walters. Harriet had been a member of the church for more than thirty years. For some twenty years she'd served as choir director. She, too, complained to Jim that his preaching was negative, and she spread her opinion around the congregation. As Jim analyzed things, it appeared that Harriet and Ellis were at the center of larger conflicts that had emerged early on between Jim and the congregation over his ministry style.

In time Jim found that he could get along well with Ellis and work out shared understandings with him—including "agreeing to disagree." But such agreements lasted only so long as Harriet wasn't "in Ellis' ear." As soon as Harriet entered the picture, Ellis would take her side.

After seeing this pattern repeat itself again and again, Jim reevaluated his assumptions about Ellis. He was accustomed to thinking of Ellis as a powerful leader in the congregation, a kind of patriarch. But now he began to consider that perhaps the fact of Ellis' wealth, though influential as wealth tends to be, had led him to attribute more authority to Ellis than Ellis really had. When Jim thought about how Ellis related to other parents in the church—and especially to Harriet—it appeared that Ellis was functioning more like a parental child than like a parent.

For one thing, few of Jim's conflicts with Ellis ever originated with Ellis himself. For example, Ellis might give Jim some critical feedback if they were out to lunch together. They would talk about it and part company on good terms, even if they hadn't reached agreement. Then Sunday morning would find Ellis irritated about one of the issues they'd talked through at lunch. He wouldn't have anything new to say, but his irritation would be fresh, and his views would be uncompromising. Jim would eventually discover that the only new element was that Harriet had been talking to Ellis (and to others). She was upset, so Ellis was upset and worried, and both were worried that other people were upset.

Many people in the congregation deferred to Ellis. On the surface he looked like the dominating patriarch in the church family. But Ellis could be strong only so long as he was certain that he was following the lead of Harriet or someone else in the close circle of his church parents. He was a church patriarch of sorts: a parental-child patriarch.

We will examine Ellis' parental style more closely in the next chapter in looking at styles of authority in the church family. Analyzing these styles will help us understand how informal parental power is used in the church family system, which in turn will give us insight into the family dynamics of church conflict.

Chapter Three

❖

Church Family Authority

Everyone was afraid of Lucy Thurber, including her pastor, Arnelle Richards. Otherwise Lucy would never have been made Bible School Director.

But during Bible School the second summer of Arnelle's pastorate, Arnelle got a different picture of Fairview Presbyterian and Lucy Thurber. Lucy openly criticized the teachers and the students. She also told two mothers that their boys were undisciplined and accused them of being greedy thieves. One of the boys, Lucy alleged, was also a sexual pervert and had made an advance on his teacher. These boys were in Arnelle's class, and none of the accusations matched what Arnelle had observed about them.

When the mothers complained to Arnelle, she encouraged them to stand up to Lucy and confront her. They would not. Arnelle called Lucy and tried to make an appointment to clear things up. Lucy was too busy. Arnelle felt powerless and angry.

The tension continued for six months. People began to confide in Arnelle about similar incidents with Lucy in the past. Many confessed that they were afraid of Lucy.

Then nominating time came around. The nominating committee had heard from Lucy that she wanted to be an elder. To avoid her wrath, the committee planned to nominate her, even though each of its members agreed with Arnelle that Lucy wasn't qualified to be an elder.

The nominating committee met one Sunday after church at the front of the sanctuary. Lucy and her husband stayed after the service, seating themselves a few rows back to observe the meeting. Here's what happened:

Laurie (chair of the committee): There are two vacancies for elder. Do we have any nominations?

Sherri: Laurie and Earl have done a great job on the board. I think we should put them back on.

Several members of the board nodded "yes." Then Lucy spoke. She had scooted up to the back of a pew so that she could see everyone. Her face was flushed and her hands were fidgeting.

Lucy: I would like to be considered for elder. I am free to attend the presbytery meetings in Omaha, and we haven't had a representative there in a long time. I've served this church in many capacities, and I think I should be considered.

Sherri: Oh, that sounds like a good idea. You'd be a good elder.

Arnelle: (heart pounding and trying to keep her voice from shaking) I'd like to say something. Lucy, you've been a valuable part of this community. You've consistently helped, served in a variety of ways, and the church appreciates all your efforts. But an elder's main purpose is to nurture the congregation and to promote the peace and unity of the congregation. Based on past experience, I don't think you're qualified to be an elder.

Lucy: If this is related to that other event, I thought we'd settled that. *(pause with no response from the committee or Arnelle)* And I'll tell you, we're going to see about this. *(pause and again no response)* You'd better just reconsider the rest of the offices we've accepted, because we're going to leave this church.

Having made this threat, Lucy summoned her husband and they stormed out. The committee decided to postpone any more decisions until the following Sunday. Over the next few weeks Arnelle's interpretation of the event enlarged as she began to discover ways in which people's attitudes toward her had been changed by it. She felt more like the pastor of Fairview than ever before. What she didn't realize was that she had become more than pastor. She was now a central parent in the family.

Church conflicts occur over issues, but they also take place over power itself. People use power when they fight over things they want, and one of the things people want is power. Lucy fights with Arnelle because Arnelle threatens her power. Arnelle acquires parental authority as a result of taking Lucy on. In this chapter we examine one central form of family power, namely parental authority. We look at the different styles of authority that church parents use, and we show how these different styles affect the dynamics of a conflict.

Parental Authority in the Church Family

The parental structure of a family is the way that the family distributes authority. Authority is one form of power.

It is the recognized right to decide for the group. It holds sway without coercion or persuasion, which are forms of power but not authority. Those with (or without) authority may use persuasion or coercion, but authority is the acknowledged right to decide for others and therefore doesn't need force or arguments to exert power. It is recognized power—power that is regarded as legitimate.

People often think of leadership as implying some sort of hierarchy. But the term *hierarchy* suggests "ruling" (*archein*), which is only one kind of leadership. "Hierarchy" often implies as well that a privileged class ought to rule. In order to avoid both these associations, we shall refer to leadership structure, which may assume any number of forms, some hierarchical.

All forms of parental authority entail some structure of dependence. But there are different kinds of dependence, and not all are found within parental leadership structures. Independent persons, for example, can learn from each other and depend on each other without one being in the position of child and the other in the role of parent. This sort of independence in mutuality ought to characterize all nonparental relations in the congregation. Parental authority entails a different structure of dependence. The child does not exercise independence in decision making and carrying out responsibility but depends on the parent for instructions.

Cultural analyst Richard Sennett has provided an extremely helpful interpretation of authority in modern Western culture.[1] Sennett's analysis turns out to be especially revealing of how familial metaphors have defined our understanding and experience of authority in American culture. Since American churches mirror American culture in so many respects, Sennett's study also sheds light on what we will call familylike authority in the congregation. Some brief descriptions of Sennett's analysis of authority in modern Western culture may provide a helpful framework for understanding the examples of authority in church families that follow.

Sennett thinks that modern, industrialized society has made a shift from paternalism as the predominant mode of exercising power to what he terms autonomism: the authority of the autonomous figure. Although both are forms of male-dominant authority, they stand in relation to each other at opposite poles.

As a pure type, paternalism is domination by a controlling form of care that does not nurture. By contrast, autonomism is domination without care. It is a psychologically detached way of managing people that makes them emotionally dependent on "fathers" who refuse to behave in fatherly ways.

A third style of authority, not discussed by Sennett but prevalent in congregational systems, is maternalism. As a pure type, maternalism is caregiving authority through enmeshment. Maternalistic parents can be as controlling, within their own more limited sphere, as paternalistic ones, but without the psychological independence that the paternalistic parent possesses.

A fourth style of authority is nurturance. Nurturance is care, support, and teaching that helps the other person to grow and achieve greater independence. Nurturing parents teach without dominating. They practice unselfish, other-centered support without sacrificing their own identities in the process.

In what follows we contrast these four styles and argue that congregational parents ought to cultivate nurturance as a predominant habit of authority and use the other three styles stintingly as certain occasions may demand.

Nurturance

For many days of training, gymnastics coach Susan Jefferson provides support with her hands for Lydia Toms as Lydia goes through the motions of a new tumbling exercise. She also listens when Lydia wants to try it a different way. They experiment together. Then one day Susan steps back. While she keeps strengthening Lydia with words of encouragement, her hands no longer supply support—except to clap when Lydia succeeds.

Nurturing parents are good coaches. They provide a careful mix of support and disengagement calculated to promote their children's growth to maturity.

The form of dependence fostered by nurture might be called dependence in mutuality. It is not static dependency. Nurturance encourages the other's growth toward independence. It is a form of care and teaching that includes the message, "I want you to grow to be independent of me, so that we become equal partners." And just as important is a second message: "I will not decide for you when you are ready to take a step toward greater independence; we'll decide together, and you, too, have a right to take the lead in that decision."

Mutuality means that both sides are active. The nurturing parent encourages the child to take steps of leadership. The fact that the child needs this encouragement from a parent is what makes the child a child. It lies in the power of the parent to initiate and foster mutuality as a bridge from dependence to independence for the child. Nurture gradually erodes the dependence of the child on the parent until the child reaches maturity as a co-adult. In the congregational family system, that means maturity as a co-parent or independent child (recall chapter 2).

If nurture were to succeed simultaneously with all congregational children, there would be no more parents. This is the paradox of parental nurture. It aims to produce more parents in the church family, but if it should succeed fully it would eliminate the category of congregational parent altogether. Nurture aims at the utopia where there are only mature and independent children under the parenthood of God.

Because it depends on mutuality, parental nurture always begins with an invitation. Arnelle extended such an invitation to Laurie after the incident with Lucy and the nominating committee. After Lucy Thurber departed, the three women who made up the nominating committee came to Arnelle to ask how she was feeling and to talk over what had happened. Laurie blurted out to Arnelle, "I'm such a coward! I left you to say that all by yourself. I'm sorry." She probably expected Arnelle to tell her it was O.K. But Arnelle smiled and agreed, "You're right, Laurie. But I think you can learn how to speak your mind to Lucy, and I'm ready to help you and support you in learning how."

This is an invitation to provide nurture. Laurie is already in a relationship of dependence on Arnelle. The question is whether it will be a dependence in mutuality on which Arnelle can build in nurturing ways. Arnelle can't make Laurie an independent child, much less a co-parent. Laurie must accept the invitation to receive nurturing rather than rescuing care. That acceptance would be itself a first step toward independence.

Paternalism

In fact Arnelle did not respond to Laurie in the way just described. Instead she said: "Laurie, I'm the pastor. It was my responsibility to say no. It would have been wrong for me to sit by and allow Lucy to become elder." This response was paternalistic. Instead of supporting Laurie to take steps toward assuming a parental role in the church family, Arnelle rescued Laurie from her responsibility. This is not to say that Laurie was really asking for encouragement to become more self-dependent. She probably assumed that Arnelle would absolve her of responsibility.

Whether practiced by a man or a woman, authority that takes responsibility away from others and thus keeps them from growing up is paternalistic. Paternalism is based on the assumption that some people are better off remaining dependent on parents who "know what's best" for them. In a patriarchal or male-dominated society, it is men who serve as the final parental authority. Women may act in paternalistic ways toward children, but "fathers" determine what is best for all.

Today paternalism in church and society is under attack, and in some congregations it is in the process of being dismantled. The Christian feminist movement has led many denominations to affirm commitment to women's ordination, and local congregations are becoming increasingly willing to change official church structures to admit women into leadership roles traditionally reserved for men.

Nevertheless, a church may admit women to all the church offices and still function as a family according to the old paternalistic hierarchy. It may follow a principle of mutuality and partnership in the way it structures its offices, boards, and committees, yet remain authoritarian in its unofficial family structure. In fact, the leadership may create this contradiction between official and unofficial patterns of authority in order to keep official authority from gaining power over the unofficial family network of power. Shiloh Baptist Church offers an example.

In 1987 Clayton Tinder, pastor and founder of Shiloh, decided to make "the priesthood of all believers" his ministry theme. Clayton had founded the Shiloh congregation with a handful of people in 1972. Over the years the church had grown to a membership of 400 and a worshiping attendance of 125. In 1984, Clayton (then at age fifty) enrolled in a nearby seminary and began working toward an M.Div. degree. By the fall of '86, he was so worn out from the combination of school, pastoral duties, and an additional job as chaplain in a local hospital that he felt he had to have help.

The church wasn't prepared to hire an associate, so Clayton decided to train members of his congregation to carry out some of the work he'd been doing. His focus on "the priesthood of all believers" grew out of reflection on his ministry predicament in the light of what he was learning in seminary.

It is fair to say that when Clayton began teaching the folks at Shiloh about the priesthood of believers, he himself was running virtually everything in the church, from chairing almost all the boards and committees to supervising the maintenance of the building. After two years of working to train lay leadership, redefine his pastoral role, and distribute responsibility and authority to others in the congregation, Clayton was still extremely frustrated. He complained that he still had to "do everything" because his new leadership "doesn't follow through." In his view "the pastor is expected to just give, give, give, without receiving any help." Clayton complained, "I still haven't got any real leaders."

An analysis of the congregational family system told a somewhat different story. Invoking his theme of the priesthood of all believers, Clayton would convene a "Church Family Business Meeting" every Sunday after church. He also called this the "Church Council." "Everyone," Clayton insisted, "from the youngest to the oldest can speak and be heard at these meetings." When the Council conducted its business in this forum of the whole, the pastor would preside, if he was present. In his absence the chair of the Deacon Board or some other church officer would preside. Although there were numerous other boards and committees in the church, most decisions were made by a majority vote of the Church Council, which met more frequently than any other group.

One Saturday afternoon in January, Clayton went over to the church building for a Deacon Board meeting and found it freezing cold. The chairman of the Deacon Board had already been there for about an hour. Clayton couldn't understand why he hadn't reset the furnace thermostat, so it would ignite. Five persons had keys to the furnace room: Al and Clayton, Henry, Calvin, and Louis. "Some of you live two or three blocks from the church," Clayton would complain. "Why don't you come over and make sure the furnace is on if you know we're going to have a meeting?"

Sometimes in the fall or early spring the opposite would happen. It would get hot in the sanctuary during Sunday service because the furnace was on.

Clayton: Nobody does anything. Four of them have keys, but they all just sit there.

Cosgrove: Maybe it's unclear to them whose job it is, which one of them is supposed to take care of it. I'm asking, Where are they during worship, where do they sit?

Clayton: Al's in the choir, Henry's with the deacons.

Cosgrove: Where do the deacons sit?

Clayton: Up front on the right.

Cosgrove: And the others?

Clayton: Calvin's an usher, and Louis is on the platform with me. He's one of the preachers.

Cosgrove: So do maybe Al and Henry and Louis feel like it would be awkward or disruptive if they got up, say, in the middle of the service to turn down the heat?

Clayton: I end up leaving the pulpit and going down to take care of it. You know, I look out at them and it's so hot they can hardly stay awake, you know, and I tell them, "It's getting awful warm in here and it isn't the fire of the Spirit." You know, I say something like that, and then I go down.

Cosgrove: But maybe Al and Henry and Louis are thinking that Calvin should be taking care of it because he's—he's an usher, so he's in the back of the church, right?

Clayton: Right.

Cosgrove: So maybe they're thinking he should be taking care of it. Maybe it's not clear whose job it is, so each one is assuming someone else is in a better position to take care of it, you know. Maybe it should be Calvin's job, but he's not clear on that. He doesn't necessarily have his key that morning?

Clayton: He's got his key.

Cosgrove: Or they are frustrated with you and so not taking care of some of these things is—you know, they just don't do them as a little form of protest?

Clayton: There you are.

Cosgrove: Do you think they may be irritated in part because, when the assignments of responsibility are not clear, each one feels like he's responsible? You're always saying to them as a group, "Why didn't one of you do this or that?" So each one maybe gets the message that everything like that is—he's responsible for everything in your eyes? But he's also able to say it's not just his job. Why doesn't one of the others do it this time? I'm just trying to look at it from their point of view.

Clayton: I think you're probably right. But they have to take some responsibility for themselves. I can't tell them everything.

Although Clayton used the language of shared responsibility, he didn't see to it that the responsibilities were divided up as clear assignments. That frustrated people. Everyone was responsible, and therefore any individual could conclude on any occasion, "It's not my job. Let someone else do it this time." This also meant that when someone acted authoritatively, Clayton (if he didn't like what was done) could claim that the person didn't have the authority.

One Sunday the pastor was in a private conference during the first part of the Church Council meeting. The matter of a bill for unapproved expenses incurred at a fund-raising event came before the Council. One of the deaconesses, Cecelia, wanted to have approval of payment tabled until the pastor arrived. Al, as chair of the board, finally suggested that they go ahead and approve payment. When Clayton found out, he was angry that Al hadn't waited for him.

Cosgrove: But didn't the Church Council have the right to settle the matter without you?

Clayton: Everything related to finances goes through me.

Cosgrove: What about the Trustee Board? Why didn't it go to the trustees?

Clayton: We had a problem with our treasurer embezzling money, and so now everything is voted on at the Church Council.

Cosgrove: So what do the trustees do? Do they have anything to do?

Clayton: No, they really don't have any responsibilities right now.

Although Clayton sought to develop and empower lay leadership by forming the Church Council, the effect was to undercut the leadership of those serving on boards and committees. Clayton gave to the leadership of the unofficial family structure, in which he served as founding father and patriarch, official authority over all the official structures of leadership in the church. It seemed like an affirmation of the priesthood of all believers when he would say "Everyone has a voice here" and when he would insist that all decisions be voted on by the gathered family, both adults and their children. But in fact, because the family regarded Clayton as their father and would defer to him more readily than to anyone else, he retained all the power (and all the burdensome responsibility) that he possessed before initiating his new plans for shared leadership.

Almost. The fact that the Church Council under the leadership of Al had begun to act independently of Clayton suggests that Clayton's work was bearing some fruit. If there was a bit of rebellion, Clayton should have welcomed it as a sign of the very egalitarianism he had been encouraging under the slogan "the priesthood of all believers."

When Clayton came to admit that his establishment of the amorphous Church Council was in fact allowing him to perpetuate his own paternalistic control over the congregation, he formed a new Church Council out of the chairs and presidents of the various boards and organizations of the church. The idea was to give leadership over to this body. This would eliminate the unclarity in having a Church Council composed at any given meeting of whoever happened to be present to attend the Church Family Business Meeting after the Sunday service. According to the new arrangement, the Church Council would meet three Tuesday evenings a month, and the Church Family Business Meeting would be held on the remaining Tuesday. Now, however, the purpose of the Church Family Business Meeting was not to conduct church business but only to hear reports of actions taken by the Council.

Cosgrove: The Church Council is now made up of chairpersons and presidents of the different boards and organizations?

Clayton: Right.

Cosgrove: And who presides over the Council meetings?

Clayton: I do.

Cosgrove: Uh-huh. How do people acquire positions like chair or president of this or that group in the church?

Clayton: By appointment.

Cosgrove: Who makes the appointments?

Clayton: I do.

Cosgrove: So you still have all the power.

Clayton: (*smiling*) O.K., I see what you're getting at.

Cosgrove: If you want to foster a more egalitarian structure of leadership, why don't you let the church as a whole elect people to the Council and let them form a nominating committee on which you don't serve?

Clayton: I could do that.

It's hard for a parent to give up power. Clayton was having difficulty letting his "children" grow up, despite his best intentions. His own divided feelings led him to send them double messages. He would use the rhetoric of egalitarianism and shared leadership, but his own family behavior often contradicted his words. And sometimes his actions were contradictory.

Perhaps the most important lesson in the Shiloh story is that the very leaders who support change away from hierarchy in the official structure may continue to maintain hierarchical patterns of power in the unofficial family system. This is especially insidious, since those who function, for example, as authoritarian patriarchs in the family system, may be themselves very cooperative in reshaping the official structures of the church to make them more egalitarian. And they may prefer a system that spreads authority among many boards and committees, without lodging too much power in a central board. Diluted authority in the official structure only means more power for them through their "family" influence.

In fact, unless Clayton nurtures leadership among others in the congregation or unless there is a significant rebellion by the "parental children" at Shiloh, it may not matter what governing system Clayton puts into effect. Under any system he can retain paternalistic power. The very fact that Clayton can change the governing systems almost at will is a testimony to his parental authority. Ironically, he can turn the church into a democracy and still remain king.

Autonomism

Paternalism is a form of "caring" authority, but it makes care a nonnegotiable gift. It often speaks, in effect, something like this: "I decide what's best for you, and you can take it or leave it (although we both know you'll take it)." And unlike nurturance, paternalistic care reinforces dependency rather than promotes growth and mature independence. In contrast to paternalistic authority, autonomous authority makes no pretense of care but works by a different strategy.

By way of illustration, Sennett presents a well-known business-management case study in which a physics research worker, Dr. Richard Dodds, shows a letter to his superior, Dr. Blackman. The letter is an offer to Dodds of a position at another research institution. The conversation begins with Dodds talking about the offer. He assures his boss that he's really happy where he is, and tries to make it clear that while he thinks he should visit the other lab, that doesn't necessarily mean he's made up his mind to leave. The conversation continues with Blackman coolly giving reasons why Dodds might want to stay on and Dodds fishing for either an affirmation, a promise of a raise, or (probably) both. After growing frustration, Dodds finally complains:

> *Dodds:* Look, I came in here, and I want to be honest with you, but you go and make me feel all guilty, and I don't like that.

> *Blackman:* You are being as honest as can be.

> *Dodds:* I didn't come in here to fight. I don't want to disturb you.

> *Blackman:* I'm not disturbed. If you think that it is best for you to go somewhere else, that is O.K. with me.

The discussion goes on a while longer until Dodds exclaims in exasperation:

> *Dodds:* I don't understand you. . . . All I wanted was to show you this letter, and let you know what I was going to do. What should I have told you?

> *Blackman:* That you had read the letter and felt that under the circumstances it was necessary for you to pay a visit to Wilkin (*the professor at the other institution*),

but that you were happy here, and wanted to stay at least until you had got a [piece] of work done.

Dodds: I can't get over it. You think there isn't a place in the world I'd rather be than here in this lab. . . .[2]

Throughout the conversation, Blackman projects an attitude of reasoned detachment. He doesn't simply keep his cool; he gives no hint that he is in any way emotionally involved in the discussion. And precisely in this way, by this strategy, he exercises emotional influence.

Nevertheless, the role Blackman plays is not simply that of the autonomous authority figure. Blackman is, in fact, in a parental role, but he refuses to acknowledge it. That's what infuriates Dodds, who ends up feeling frustrated and guilty. Blackman isn't paternalistic, at least not straightforwardly so. He is a boss who uses the psychological power he possesses as a father without acting like a father. Yet his fatherly power is really at work in the relationship, as Dodds' emotional reactions make clear. But that power seems invisible, as if it comes from nowhere. So there's no way for Dodds to get at it. Paradoxically, Blackman plays the role of an absent father.

When we have shared the exchange between Dodds and Blackman with women pastors, their response has been very negative toward Blackman. By contrast, men in executive positions tend to evaluate Blackman positively and regard Dodds as an emotionally manipulative person. In fact, the Dodds-Blackman exchange is used in management training as a model of how to handle difficult employees.[3]

Granted that Dodds may be manipulative and in some ways childish and that there are times when it is appropriate to assume an emotionally detached style of leadership, autonomy is itself manipulative. As a primary style of leadership, it is inhumane. It uses the emotional energy that always exists in human relationships but acts as if human relationships are themselves unimportant, as if only rationality and the task at hand counts for anything.

If cultural forms of authority tend to insinuate themselves into the church, then we should expect to find an increase in the use of autonomous authority in congregations today. In fact, the autonomistic style of authority is one that church leaders do spontaneously adopt as a strategy of influence in the church.

You have to be in a parental role in order to succeed at autonomism. The way you play the game of autonomous authority is to keep your emotions hidden, resist expressing any care (even when you give advice and even when you voice "caring concern"), and put everything on what appears to be a purely rational plane. Our culture has trained males, above all, to cultivate the autonomous identity that supports this style.

To judge from his self-descriptions, Steve Adams tended to adopt the autonomous style of authority when he was under pressure and feared losing control. Let's look at how he describes his own behavior during the fateful meeting to reorganize the choir:

> I spoke to them about what ministry is and how I viewed them as ministers. They were proclaiming the gospel just like I was on Sunday mornings. There's a certain responsibility and need for commitment. And Jack kept interrupting me before I got to the actual conflict. I basically said it seems like we have two options with the choir. Either we can disband, because it seems like some people want to quit, and we need people to have a choir. Or we

can reorganize and become more disciplined and work on how we function as a choir. From that point on the meeting degenerated. People started yelling, making accusations, and I lost total control.

This report is Steve's reconstruction from memory, and it is evident that he is trying both to be frank and also to cast himself in a favorable light. As he describes it, just about everyone gets emotional except him. People yell, interrupt one another, and make accusations, while Steve remains calm and tries to put everything on a rational level.

Steve is no doubt idealizing his own role in the meeting, but his ideal turns out to be what we have described as the autonomous authority style. He makes no statements of pastoral empathy but instead offers comments and observations devoid of warmth. His last few statements are especially revealing. He presents the "two options" (disband the choir or reorganize) as if he personally doesn't care what the group does. And the response of people to his emotional and rational detachment is anger—although it's not all aimed at him. In fact, one reason why it is not all directed at him is that he's not a parent in this setting. Which is also why his strategy of autonomism does not succeed. Autonomism works only for persons who already possess parental authority with those they want to influence. But Steve is not regarded as a father by the choir. He's an independent child; hence, the choir members don't pay much attention to him but fight among themselves instead.

Maternalism

One Wednesday morning in March, Jim Roper got a call at home from Harriet Walters (recall chapter 2). A light snow was falling, and Harriet was worried that the weather would be too treacherous for people coming to choir practice that night. She hinted that maybe they should cancel choir practice. Should she start calling around? Jim suggested that she wait and see. "But what about Muriel Jensen and the Larsons?" Harriet fretted. "Well, they can decide whether to come or not," Jim said, adding, "Just because you are the one who calls choir practice doesn't mean you're responsible for their decision whether they can come or not."

But Jim knew that Harriet was going to worry all day until either the snow stopped and the roads cleared or she called off practice. Jim decided that if the phone rang again, he'd let his answering machine take the call. He didn't want to communicate with Harriet again that morning.

It wasn't that Jim couldn't talk to Harriet or work out differences with her. It was that he didn't like contact with her. Conversation with Harriet was work for him and often left him a bit drained. When there was a conflict between them, dealing with it would exhaust him. As much as he was able, he avoided her.

We asked Jim to use family metaphors to name the roles he and Harriet played in the congregation. He judged that they were both parents. "Harriet's a mother—a powerful mother," he said. And once he had named her role, it dawned on him that in part what tired him so much in relating to Harriet was this. It felt like she was always trying to mother him and in ways that he found manipulative or smothering, sometimes both. So when he and Harriet interacted, Jim was always expending extra energy to keep from being "controlled" and "cared for" by her.

A third style of authority is maternalism. Maternalism is maternal authority extended through relationships with men who have authority. Sometimes these relationships involve enmeshment. They always entail emotional dependence. By caring for another person self-sacrificially, the mother creates a dependence that gives her power. And that power gives her some control of whatever authority the other person possesses. Thus maternalism is a combination of maternal authority and power over male authority. This combination makes the maternalistic style of authority more complex than paternalism or autonomism. In order to understand how it works, we must first examine maternal authority itself.

Maternal authority is the authority that the mother has traditionally possessed within the family home. As such it is a household authority based on what have been traditionally conceived as the mother's special areas of natural competence in the family: care for the children and management of household work (sometimes including the control of the household purse).

A dominant theme in this traditional conception of the woman's role in the household is that mother speaks definitively in matters of feeling. She is the recognized authority over the sphere of the emotions—at least those that count within the family circle. A perusal of American magazines such as *The Saturday Evening Post* published before the American media's accommodation to feminism confirms this image. Wherever she is found (almost always in the home, of course) mother radiates the reassuring and sometimes even sensuous beauty of emotional competence in love, care, and tenderness.

Upon feeling too limited by the confines of maternal authority, women in maternal roles sometimes seek to enlarge their power by cultivating emotional power over men. This extension of maternal authority produces maternalism.

Not long after Jim Roper began his ministry at Evergreen Community Church, Harriet began complaining about his preaching. What Jim himself regarded as a bold and pro-phetic elucidation of the gospel, Harriet described as "too negative." She began worrying about how it was making her "children" feel. Harriet enlisted Ellis' help to get Jim to modify his preaching. When she and Ellis failed to persuade Jim to change, Ellis invited a denominational leader (male) to talk to Jim about his preaching. If Ellis did so because Harriet suggested it, then we have an example of maternal-ism. Harriet's maternal authority does not extend beyond the church household. As a woman she would have diffi-culty persuading a male denominational leader to intervene. But Ellis has considerable authority not only within but also outside the church family. And thanks to Ellis' dependence on her, Harriet is able to extend her maternal power to spheres of influence otherwise inaccessible to her.

Maternalism is typically a woman's mode of parental power in our society. Although it shares features in common with paternalism, it does not stand on the same level with either the paternalistic or the autonomous style. It is a mode of power built up from below, a result of the cultural sup-pression of women. By its very nature, it is not suited to gaining and maintaining official power in society. And the only way in which it exercises influence in official and public centers of authority is through surrogates (for exam-ple, a maternalistic wife controlling a husband who enjoys authority in the marketplace, the church, the political arena, etc.).

It is very important to recognize the cultural limitations imposed on maternalistic authority. People sometimes argue that because of their "influence over men," women have always exercised power in all spheres of life and have never really been subordinated to male authority. Some go so far as to suggest that women have possessed the "real" power all along. Women can manipulate men psychologically, they say, since women enjoy special competence in the world of human emotions in relationship.

This way of construing women's traditional power misses several crucial facts. First, by no means can all men be manipulated emotionally. In fact, the male tendency toward individuation, as evidenced in both the paternalistic and autonomous modes of authority, protects men against emotional control. For example, when Jim thought Harriet was trying to manipulate him emotionally, he would instinctively shift into autonomism and keep her at a distance through emotionally detached "reasoning." And that's exactly how he treated her when she called that Wednesday morning to worry him about the possibility of a snowstorm.

Maternalistic power over male authority is "circumstantial." It depends on the particular man and the circumstances of the relationship. It is not a socially recognized power of women over "men" as a class.

Second, no amount of prowess in the politics of the emotional life can change the fact that women have historically been blocked by men from social positions of authority and that this inaccessibility to social authority has severely limited women's power.

Most important, this false argument about women having the "real power" makes the mistake of confusing power with authority. Men and women can exercise emotional power over one another, but men have not needed to use their influence over the women in their life in order to acquire authority outside the sphere of the family household. By contrast, until the rise of modern feminism— which is a cultural revolution still in progress—women as a class did not enjoy authority in the public sphere. And this has held true for women in the church, a sphere in which women in Protestant America have enjoyed considerable power without socially recognized authority, namely, the circumstantial power over male authority they manage to gain through maternalism.

Maternalism and Co-dependence

Because maternalistic authority depends on sacrificial caregiving and has only a limited independent basis of power, it is sometimes found together with the emotional addiction known as co-dependence.

Co-dependence is a form of emotional dependency based on low self-esteem and diffuse self-identity. In our society, the co-dependent is typically a woman.[4] She derives her identity almost entirely from others: her husband, children, church—any persons, organizations, or institutions that she perceives can lend her a sense of vicarious worth. She seeks identity through enmeshment and tries to find self-worth by becoming indispensable to others. She attaches herself to people and causes. She is a chronic church volunteer.[5] She is driven to do whatever others say is needed because she has no self-confidence out of which to decide for herself what is needful.

She aims to please, exhausts herself in trying to please. When someone else is unhappy, she assumes that it's her own fault. She redoubles her efforts. Pleasing others is the only way she knows of making herself count, and when it fails she tries again. Afraid of being cut off from others and left to herself, she becomes addicted to relationship. She clings. Because she devotes all her mind and heart to discerning the feelings and needs of others, in order to make herself count by counting to them, she is cut off from her own feelings. She imagines that by giving she will acquire a sense of well-being and self-value. Because she is caught in one-way patterns of attending to others without receiving reciprocal understanding, she may feel lonely.

Harriet Walters is a maternalistic parent. She also shows many signs of being co-dependent with her church and with her various church children. Spending all day worrying about whether to cancel choir practice because it might not stop snowing is typical of her. When she expends her excessive care on Jim, he feels hemmed in. But at least some of her children enjoy the diffuse sea of her maternal love.

One should not devalue the work Harriet does or all of the care she gives. But it is important to see how her style of authority—a style that she has been encouraged by her society and church world to cultivate—hinders her self-formation. Because she is always seeking her value and identity in others, she never arrives at her own self.[6]

Authority Styles as a Parental Repertoire

Maternalism does not always entail co-dependence. Nor does the exercise of maternal authority always take the form of maternalism. For instance, a woman who functions as a parent in a patriarchal (nonegalitarian) church family possesses maternal authority. She may not be enmeshed with any of her children. In fact, she may treat her children in a paternalistic way, but that does not mean she enjoys paternal authority in the family. So it is useful to distinguish, at least to some extent, the different styles of authority from the three basic kinds of authority that a parent may possess: maternal, paternal, or simply parental.[7] While possessing a single kind of authority, a person may employ more than one of the four styles.

Thus one will find women using different styles of authority in the church family. Some may exercise maternal authority in a paternalistic way, others may do so in a maternalistic way. Some of the maternalistic ones may tend toward enmeshment or even be in co-dependent relationships with others. Some of the paternalistic ones may also use the autonomous style.

In fact, the four styles of authority we have described can be practiced by both men and women. Just as women can adopt a paternalistic or autonomistic style of authority, so men can adopt a maternalistic style. A man can behave like a mother (in the maternalistic sense) just as a woman can behave like a father (in the paternalistic sense).

Not only that, there are occasions when any one of these styles may be the most appropriate. In fact, while we advocate nurturance as the routine style of authority for congregational parents, we recognize that this style can deform into nurturism if practiced without any regard to circumstances.

There are times when it is important for the good of the other person or the good of the family—and times when it is simply morally right—that a parent should adopt one of the other three styles.

Prophets, for example, must do more than nurture. There is an inherently paternalistic element in prophetic authority owing to the fact that in the end prophets must be willing to speak and act regardless of the readiness or even the willingness of others to heed them. When doing what is right must take priority over the right of self-determination by the individual or the group, the parent has no recourse but to exercise authority in a paternalistic way.

Occasionally, it is also necessary to use an autonomous style of authority. When the nurturing approach confronts attempts at emotional manipulation, the nurturer-coach ought to adopt an autonomous style. By way of example, let's imagine Blackman and Dodds in a church setting instead of a research lab. Let's make Blackman a senior pastor in a large church and Dodds an assistant pastor on his staff. In a conversation like the one reported earlier, pastor Blackman might have employed the autonomous style and still given Dodds genuine support. In the transcript Blackman says at one point: "I'm not disturbed. If you think that it is best for you to go somewhere else, that is O.K. with me." He might have said: "Richard, I'm glad you came to talk to me about this, and I do want you to stay with us. But I'm ready to support you if you think it's best for you to go elsewhere. Let me be frank; I'm not prepared to campaign to get you a raise, if that's what you have in mind. But we can discuss it."

Sometimes empathy and care for another person must have priority over all other considerations. Then it's right to be maternalistic by letting go of oneself and becoming immersed in the concerns of the other.

Let's imagine another day and another conversation between assistant pastor Dodds and senior pastor Blackman. The two have discussed plans for an upcoming church event; it's time for Dodds to be on his way. But he loiters in Blackman's office doorway, prolonging the conversation in a way that is beginning to irritate Blackman. Then, just when Blackman is about to end their chat, Dodds blurts out, "My daughter has leukemia; we just found out." Blackman, who routinely works out of the autonomous mode of authority, is at a loss to respond adequately. He is not wired to be able to forget himself and speak words that comfort like a mother's arms, perhaps even to embrace Dodds. But in this moment an autonomistic, paternalistic, or even nurturing style of authority is not called for. It is a time only for the gift of one's being to sustain another.

We are convinced that the nurturing style of parental authority ought to be the preferred and routine style used by congregational parents. But we make an important distinction between a routine nurturing style of authority and nurturism. Nurturing authority is an everyday habit of authority, from which a parent may occasionally depart under certain circumstances. It turns into nurturism only when it becomes a frozen mode of being practiced by a parent who is too inflexible to use other styles when they are appropriate. The problem with nurturism is that it leaves the parent vulnerable to emotional manipulation and unwilling to make unpopular moral decisions. It also makes one blind to crisis needs, those occasions when another person really is, at least for the moment, helpless. Crisis usually calls for a response of parental self-abandon, not the calculated support of the nurturing coach.

As habitual styles of authority, paternalism, autonomism, and maternalism inhibit the growth of others, and when we hinder others from maturing, we aren't behaving like mature parents. Therefore, nurturance is the most mature style of parental authority. The styles of paternalism, maternalism, and autonomism are all temptations to control. But there is no such temptation in nurturance, because nurturance is by definition the work of relinquishing power to others by supporting their growth and independence (in mutuality). Nurturing parents don't make control their primary aim in power relations, and therefore they can adopt a paternal, autonomous, or maternal style in certain situations, without falling into paternalism, autonomism, or maternalism.

Power, Parents, and Leadership in the Family

It is important to stress that the metaphor of dependence by congregational children on parents does not mean that in every dimension of church life the children are dependent on the parents. In the church family, the dependence of congregational children on parents has to do with leadership and decision-making functions. Parents are unofficial leaders, and parental authority within the familial order of the congregational system is a combination of ability and willingness to lead on one side and deference (by children) on the other.

This does not mean that in parity relationships (parent to parent, sibling to sibling), there is no leading and following. Parents defer to one another according to divisions of responsibility they have mutually agreed upon. But they arrive at those divisions of responsibility through negotiation as relative equals. The deference they show for one another is therefore secondary and not primary to their identity as co-parents. Not only that, children in the congregation may take turns leading among themselves, and parents may invite them to lead in various settings or even to occupy official positions.

These are important qualifications. There are many forms and instances of "leading" in the congregation. Parental leadership is only one form. While unofficial authority within the congregation resides with the parents, they do not for that reason exercise all forms of congregational leadership. Nor do they possess all the power, as we shall see.

Chapter Four

❖

Family Rules and Games

Several of the women on the Sanctuary Decorating Committee at Glendale United Methodist Church told pastor Stewart Novack that it was time to replace the faded artificial flowers at the front of the sanctuary. These were not easily accessible. Could the pastor or one of the men (like Don who lives next door) remove them? There is a ladder in a closet downstairs. Pastor Stewart is only too happy to get the ladder out and remove the flowers. He tells the women, "The old flowers are gone, so be sure to bring the new flowers for Sunday and ask one of the men to put them up." Sunday morning the eldest matriarch, Winnie, marches furiously into the pastor's office, demanding to know why the flowers she donated to the church have been removed. Not only that, why weren't they at least returned to her? She found them in the trash! Pastor Stewart apologizes but explains that the Sanctuary Decorating Committee authorized their removal. "Yes, and they're all young women," Winnie retorts. "And everyone knows those flowers were mine."

It also comes out that Winnie "gave" an organ to the church, which she plays at service every Sunday and locks up afterward with the only key, which she keeps in her possession. No one else plays Winnie's organ.

Don (from next door) later explains, "Pastor, what you did seemed right, but it wasn't right, because it offended Winnie, and we won't have her around very much longer." There is the hint of an informal rule here: Don't do anything that offends our grandmothers. And this rule overrides official authority. For sixteen years Winnie herself has been cultivating the myth, "You won't have me around much longer."

At a meeting of the Membership Committee, Lucy Cowell said she was worrying that by the time her mother died, there wouldn't be much of a church left for her mother's funeral. Stewart asked himself how statements like this and what Don had said to him might be understood in family terms. "This is a death watch," Stewart concluded. And the more he thought about it, the more this metaphor seemed to suggest a family game with its own rules.

The advent of modern psychology has encouraged us to see implicit games in everyday social interaction. People "play games" with one another, without ever naming the games or their rules. In his 1964 book, *Games People Play*, psychologist Eric Berne proposed that social life can be understood fundamentally as a set of largely unconscious games people play with one another.[1] Each game has a theme, a set of roles, its own dynamics, and its own ulterior aims. The aims are pay-offs and thus provide the incentives for people to participate in the game.

As church family systems, people play games with one another. But often they have only a dim awareness of the nature of the game they are playing or its rules. In fact, they may be able to name the rules more easily than the game itself. But even the rules may be all but out of sight.

Stewart used the metaphor of "death watch" to theorize about what game his congregation might be playing. Thinking of Death Watch as a game led him to a better understanding of how things operated in his church. According to Stewart, the game of Death Watch is about planning for our funerals.

Death Watch has several rules. Rule 1: Conserve resources so that they will be available for "funerals." In particular, this means that all those under fifty are to set aside their wants in order to be certain that the generations ahead of them have things the way they like them for their twilight years and funerals.

Rule 2: Church planning must assume the form of "funeral talk." Other talk and planning is postponed until "after." In a literal family, gathered around dying Aunt Sally's bed, you don't ask Mom if you can have a new bike next Christmas. This kind of talk would be regarded as inappropriate. Likewise in a church family playing Death Watch, you don't ask that the church provide a nursery for families like yours, which has infants and toddlers. In general you don't talk about the long-term future in the presence of the dying.

Rule 3: Don't criticize the older leadership. It is inappropriate to speak negatively about the dying. Acquiesce to their needs and desires. "Pastor, what you did seemed right, but it wasn't right because it offended Winnie, and we won't have her around very much longer."

Rule 4: Don't be too happy.

The game of Death Watch is partly literal. There are a few of the "dying" who are in fact in the last years of their lives. But Death Watch is largely a metaphor that interprets how the parents understand the present state and work of the church. On the basis of that self-understanding, they make decisions about mission, the use of family resources, planning for the future, and so forth. The pastor can wear himself out trying to generate a spirit of joy. He can align himself with· some of the younger members in proposing mission-supportive church projects. But these efforts may prove fruitless unless the parents can be coaxed into playing a new game.

"Problem People" as Clues to Unspoken Rules

The "Searchers," a young adult class at Lewisburg Presbyterian Church, had a "problem" with a man named Jerry. To most members of the class, Jerry seemed to be a very obnoxious person who was constantly making a false display of himself as multitalented and an expert on everything. Listen to what two class members say about him:

Art: Remember last week when we sang that little song, you know, at the end of the service?

Pam: You mean, "May the light of Christ shine . . ."?

Art: Right. You know what Jerry said to me after the service? He said the melody is so beautiful that he's writing a symphonic arrangement of it. Then he starts telling me about how the cellos are going to do this and the trumpets are going to go like this. Do you believe that guy!

Pam: I know; I can't stand the way he goes into those long dissertations in class like he's a biblical expert or something. I mean, practically everyone in the room is a college graduate except for him, and we even have a couple of people who are in seminary, but he acts like he knows everything.

The Searchers class was made up of college graduates. In fact, everyone had at least a bachelor's degree—except for Jerry. The class also included both married couples and single persons. Five members of the class were single women. Jerry, who was also single, had asked each of them to go out with him. Some he had asked more than once, always to be refused. The women tried to avoid him, but he would corner them at church and would sometimes speak to them in ways they found too forward. Other times he would embarrass them by things he would say in class.

Art, who is the regular teacher for the Searchers class, offers an example. One Sunday the subject for the class was "temptation." Art asked whether someone could define temptation. "Immediately," Art explains, "Jerry says that pretty legs are his definition of temptation, and then he expands on this by indicating the legs of several women in the class who were currently tempting him." "I made a joke," Art says, "and the rest of the class sort of snickered, and we just went on and ignored what Jerry said."

A systems analysis of a congregation's (or subgroup's) toleration of what it regards as unacceptable behavior by one or more of its members suggests that the problem lies not simply with the offending individuals but with the system as a whole. The offending person is often symptomatic of a problem resident in the group. Sometimes troublemakers are tolerated because the family cannot challenge them without violating one of its own rules or threatening one of its own values. Hence, when a troublemaker's place in the system is jeopardized, the system itself will often mobilize to protect the troublemaker. The very people who have been injured by the troublemaker may even come to the troublemaker's defense in one way or another, and they will do so in order to preserve the present form of the system.

During the month of May, Art was out of town for several weeks and other class members took turns teaching. Jerry wanted to know how they were chosen for this. Someone leaned over to him and said, "You have to be invited."

In fact, one not only acquired opportunities to teach by invitation only, one became a member of the class by invitation. No one had invited Jerry. He had simply started showing up. Acceptance of the unspoken rule, "participation by invitation only," made class members resent the presence of the uninvited Jerry. But they had to deal with him in a way that did not expose the rule, which contradicted both their Christian ideals and the rhetoric of the larger church family, which invited all to participate in a Sunday school class of their choice. Openly confronting Jerry would run the risk of raising the question of why he was there in the first place, and that might expose the fact that the class was really an exclusive clique.

The rule of "participation by invitation" in the Lewisburg Sunday school class really meant acceptance by invitation. If you were invited to be part of the class or to serve the class in some way, this meant that you were valued and accepted. In such an environment, the way to affirm others is to give them invitations. And if you affirm others by offering them invitations, you expect to be affirmed in return. That is the basic rule of the game. Given the presence of this unspoken rule, the way in which Jerry related to the single women in the class may perhaps be understood in a different light. It is at least worth considering that when Jerry makes repeated and inappropriate attempts to get women in the class to date him, he is following the rule: acceptance by invitation. I accept you by inviting you to go on a date with me and you owe me acceptance in return.

The preceding interpretation does not mean that the women in the class are somehow to blame for Jerry's behavior. The women, along with Jerry and the other men in the class, are part of a system that tolerates Jerry's behavior in order to protect a valued rule. The class couldn't deal honestly with Jerry's obnoxiousness and unacceptable behavior, because to have done so might have exposed the rule. The rule was more embarrassing to them than the presence of Jerry.

The "Useful" Troublemaker

The power of family rules helps explain why pastors often have so much difficulty dealing effectively with the problem of "troublemakers" in the church, those whose habitual behaviors distract from the continuing ministry of the congregation or at points directly block it. When faced with a chronic pattern of conflict due to the recurrent behaviors of a particular individual, couple, or family in the church, the pastor often discovers that the congregation as a whole treats the problem in a highly ambivalent and sometimes outright paradoxical way.

Typically the group as a whole shares in large measure the same frustrations as the pastor about the pattern of behavior in question. But just as typically the congregation seems all too willing to tolerate troublemaking rather than

to take concerted action against it. Some pastors may interpret this to mean that they and their congregations largely
agree in the diagnosis of the problem ("It's so-and-so, who
always does such-and-such") but not in its remedy: confrontation. The pastor who wants the body openly and honestly
to confront the unacceptable behavior has difficulty getting
the church and its leadership to act. And when the church
does engage the problem, it manages to do so in a way that
ultimately gives the troublemakers the leeway to continue
behaving as before. The pastor may then attribute this to a
failure of nerve owing to an inability to deal openly with
conflict. In fact many congregations do operate with a rule
that says "Christians don't fight." But at Sable Valley (recall
chapter 1), the church did confront the problem openly and
still decided in the end not even to censure John and Jane.
This suggests that other family rules were operative in
addition to "Christians don't fight." Systems will also tolerate troublemakers not only to avoid open conflict but also
because the group perceives that it derives some benefit
from the offending persons and perhaps even from their
"unacceptable" behavior. Troublemakers are sometimes tolerated because they serve a function in the system.

Shortly after his arrival as pastor of Sable Valley Community Church, people began warning Peter Wells, "Watch
out for John and Jane." Members from almost every family
of the congregation stopped by to deliver this message in
one way or another. "They starved out our first pastor, and
wore out the second." "They will drive your wife crazy, if
you let 'em!" "We don't know what to do about them; we
need their talent, work, and money. But they keep driving
people away."

Even more troubling was the frequently repeated confession, "They tricked us into getting rid of the former pastors, and we were misused. We don't want that to happen again." Ministers from neighboring congregations phoned to welcome the new pastor and to warn about John and Jane. What was one to think?

John and Jane themselves dropped by the pastor's office on Monday of his second week at Sable Valley. Smiling and gracious, they introduced themselves. "We're John and Jane Reever. We suppose you've heard about us. What have people been telling you?" Peter was taken aback, but he managed to say, "I could summarize it all by saying that you seem to be the big, bad wolf." "And what do you think about that?" John wanted to know. "I make up my own mind about people," Peter said, "and I see no reason why we can't work together."

Three years later Peter was convinced that John and Jane were wolves. He and the deacons had a long list of grievances against the couple, compiled during months of trying to work things out with John and Jane according to the Sable Valley rules of church discipline. (These rules were essentially an adaptation of Matthew 18:15-22.) At the end of a long and painful process, the deacons finally recommended to the congregation that John and Jane's membership be rescinded. They had learned that the couple, who claimed charter membership, had in fact never held membership in the church, although they had served as church officers. But this detail was only the tip of an iceberg of deception. John and Jane had lied and caused pain to many members of Sable Valley, some of whom testified publicly in the all-church meeting at which the deacons presented their recommendation.

The deacons were united with the pastor, who was well liked and respected. John and Jane had practically no friends in the church, and the evidence supporting the revocation of their now-disputed membership was more than sufficient. Yet the congregation, led by a group of vocal Retirees, voted against the recommendation of the pastor and the deacons. Peter was dumbfounded. It was only months later, when he began to reflect on his experience from a systems point of view, that it occurred to him that John and Jane did perhaps serve a purpose in the Sable Valley congregation. They drove newcomers away.

When Sable Valley Church extended its pastoral call to Peter, it was vocal in expressing its need to grow and encouraged the pastor to be evangelistic. But Peter soon learned that the membership by and large did not want to make room for strangers. Although everyone voiced support for outreach and church growth, the game behind this rhetoric was Keep the Church the Same. Peter later theorized that one unspoken rule of Keep the Church the Same was that someone be designated to drive away newcomers, so that the rest of the church could posture openness to outreach but not risk growth and change. The presence of John and Jane allowed the congregation to engage in the bad faith of supporting growth, complaining indignantly about the way John and Jane alienated potential new members, and nurturing a sense of self-righteousness about how long-suffering and forgiving they were in putting up with John and Jane.

Peter arrived at this interpretation by thinking from outcomes to intentions. In fact, John and Jane did drive newcomers away and had been doing so for several years. And the church had long tolerated this behavior, despite all the individual complaints that people made against the couple. But in the past two years, Peter had interested his deacon board and others in growing. The church took in new members, younger families joined, and soon a modest building program was underway to provide more adequate Christian education facilities. It was in the midst of this growth that people began saying that "something must be done" about John and Jane. Most of those who complained were members who were committed to opening up and expanding the church family through outreach. The Retirees did not vocally oppose growth, but they were the least enthusiastic about the programs devised by the pastor and others to foster outreach. When the church voted on the deacons' recommendations about John and Jane, the Retirees as a block opposed the recommendation. Those whom Peter named the Disreputables, along with some others, also voted against the recommendation.

Peter concluded that in the end the Retirees continued to honor the unspoken rule governing the behavior of John and Jane. He also suspected that the Disreputables and the other church family members who voted against the deacons' recommendation did so perhaps not so much because they also tacitly supported this rule but because the idea of anyone's membership being revoked threatened them. Perhaps the church's tolerance of people like John and Jane made everyone else feel secure in their own right to belong.

A Question of Strategy

Another thing that Peter Wells learned in reflecting on his Sable Valley experience from a family systems perspective is that the deacons who carried out the action against John and Jane were not parents in the church family system. Unaware of at least one key family rule and incognizant of the identity and crucial role of congregational parents outside the official systems, Peter walked blindly into a confrontation with John and Jane that he (and the deacons) could not win, even though they were in the right.

But what might Peter have done had he understood beforehand not only the function of John and Jane in the system but also the family structure that prevented the diaconate's efforts from succeeding? What can members of the Searchers class do to change their class family system? What might their pastor do to help them? What can Stewart Novack do to induce his congregation to give up Death Watch and play a more healthy, mission-centered church family game?

These are questions of strategy. We have spent these last four chapters examining the basic elements and internal dynamics of church family systems. It is now time to synthesize these learnings for practical use. The next chapter does so by bringing together everything discussed so far under a single method of analysis called "mapping." Mapping is a way of diagramming the church family, mentally and on paper. It provides the basis for devising strategies to modify the family system, which is the focus of the last three chapters of the book.

Chapter Five

❖

Mapping

M ap me no maps, sir" says one of playwright Henry Fielding's characters; "my head is a map, a map of the whole world."[1] Not everyone's head can contain the world, even if the world in question is only the small yet intricate microcosm of the congregation. That's why we draw maps. Mapping a church family helps us keep track of all the pieces and relationships that make up its familylike system. But mapping is much more than this. It is also a form of analysis that focuses the significant features of the family system, which are at play in any given family conflict or difficulty. Out of this focus come strategies for pastoral action. This chapter explains how to draw church family maps. But it is above all about the mental process of mapping. Whatever we may inscribe on paper as a way of representing our analysis of the family system, our heads are the real maps. Mapping is a way of thinking.

What to Map

A map represents the family system at a particular moment in time. It is usually most helpful to begin by mapping a typical moment of conflict in the life of the congregation. The conflict may be open or hidden. It may be a conflict that (as far as you know) only you yourself experience—perhaps a typical blockage to ministry about which you are frustrated or angry. Or it may be an experience of conflict more widely shared, whether or not all those involved have expressed their feelings and opinions openly.

To produce a map, we tell a story leading up to the chosen event or moment of conflict. Then we begin placing persons and subsystems on the map. We include the participants in the event along with any other relevant persons and subsystems, locating them above or below the parental boundary and identifying which "children" go with which "parents."

In mapping it is important to keep official and unofficial (family) systems straight. Family systems and official systems interact, and it is easy to confuse them when analyzing the systemic dynamics of a local congregation. Using the family metaphor to interpret our data helps us differentiate the two. But it is also possible and useful to employ family metaphors to interpret the official system. For example, the chairperson of the Church Council may be a child in the family system, but the office (Chair of the Council) is an official parental role. The senior minister may write a job description for a new associate that puts the associate in a subordinate and highly supervised role like that of a parental child. This, however, says nothing in itself about where that associate will end up functioning in the informal family system.

Sometimes it is helpful to draw two maps, one of the family system and one of the official structure, and to use family metaphors to interpret both and discover how they interact. At other times it is more convenient to include some official systems on the family map but to analyze them as subsystems within the family. For example, one could represent a board of elders (official parents) on a family map

by placing some above and some below the parental boundary to indicate their (unofficial) church family roles. And
suppose one discovered that all these "official parents" are
"children" in the family? That would be an illuminating
insight. It might indicate that the real authority in the
church lies hidden behind the official structure in parents
who do not seek office. Or perhaps a pastor has been so
domineering that parents have virtually abdicated all
authority, with the result that the only people who can be
persuaded to assume church offices are those who are willing
to take orders.

Symbols of Mapping

In drawing church family maps we use the following
symbols (fig. 1), some of which we have introduced already.
(See also the sample map on page 4.)

Figure 1

- - - - - - -	porous boundary
. . . .	diffuse boundary
————	rigid boundary
//	conflict (the slashes are drawn across a boundary symbol)
PC	parental child
IC	independent child
▷	triangulation
}	coalition

Every map will have a parental boundary indicated by a
central horizontal line. We begin by marking only the outer

ends of this boundary, leaving its middle segments to be filled in as we go along:

|-   -|

Persons and subsystems are shown by names or initials, and it is usually helpful to circle subsystems.

Mapping Belleville

We have already made enough tentative judgments about Steve Adams' church, Belleville Baptist (chapters 1, 2, and 3), to start mapping it as a congregational family system. We choose the choir meeting as our focal event. The key participants in this episode (see pages 30-33) and in the history leading up to it are as follows: Steve himself, Denise and Margaret (best friends), Jack (Denise's husband), the choir, Al (the director-organist), and Bill Lewis. In and around this history are other stories that shed light on the system. These stories have brought the following subsystems into view: Al's wife, Nancy, and their children, some "new oldcomers," and the congregation that extended the pastoral call to Steve (which includes everyone already named except for the newcomers).

Our analysis of the family system on the basis of what we have so far learned results in the map presented in figure 2.

The whole choir is situated below the parental boundary, indicating that none of its members is functioning as a parent. Even Denise, the quasi-official director, defers to Bill, according to Steve. A group of newcomers is

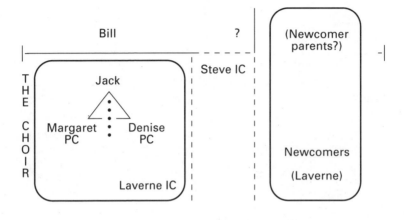

Figure 2

placed below the line. It may be that some of these persons belong above the line, but we don't have enough information yet to make a judgment. We have identified Steve as an independent child because his descriptions of his interactions with Bill indicate mutuality and independence, while his descriptions of his relationship with children in the church family suggest that he himself is not a parent.[2]

We have located Bill above the line. He is a significant parent in the congregation and the only parent we have identified thus far. We know that the choir listens to him, as do the people who attend Wednesday night Bible Study.

The boundary between Steve and Bill lies within the porous range. Their communication is basically open and unbroken. This is a very encouraging fact. Imagine the predicament Steve would be in if a rigid boundary existed between him and Bill. In that case, Steve would have no chance for constructive influence with the most significant parent in his church. Not only that, the rigid boundary would affect Steve's relation to all the children who defer to Bill as parent.

The boundary between Bill and others appears to be rigid. At least the transactions we analyzed suggest that Bill's communications with his children are basically one-way. We have therefore placed a rigid boundary also between him and the newcomers. The question mark next to this boundary indicates that this guess remains to be tested.

The boundary between Margaret and Denise is diffuse. Their tendency to communicate through Denise's husband, Jack, is also represented as "triangulation" (explained later). The "IC" next to Laverne marks her as an independent child. We have placed her on the map twice (once in parentheses) because she belongs to two subsystems represented on the map. We have marked Denise and Margaret as parental children, using the symbol "PC."

With the modest mapping we have done so far, we can already see where Steve needs to concentrate his energy: on opening up the rigid boundary between Bill and other church family members and on nurturing others in the system toward parental roles.

Guidelines for Mapping

Producing an illuminating map depends on asking the right questions and keeping the big picture of the system in view at all times. In what follows, we provide a set of guidelines for mapping, making use of family systems concepts already discussed in foregoing chapters and also introducing some new ones: coalitions, family memories, family ghosts, and triangulation.

We have arranged sixteen steps of mapping under five categories. These steps do not exhaust the relevant questions to pursue in mapping, but the list does indicate the most basic ones. In describing these steps, we use the metaphor of a game introduced in the last chapter. Since any conflict is a type of contest, the metaphor of a game is well suited to interpreting the dynamics of a congregational conflict. And it will help us explain the relationship between (a) the participants in the event, (b) family rules, and (c) the goals of those involved (which may go unspoken).

The five categories of mapping are: (1) the narrative, (2) the players, (3) the boundaries, (4) the goals and rules of the family game, and (5) tests of when mapping is complete. We also have two recommendations about the process of mapping. First, it is helpful to do mapping in an unfamiliar place. It is a basic principle of Minuchin's theory that by reconfiguring space—where people sit in a room, and so forth—one can modify perceptions and relationships. The same holds for our relationships with ourselves and with our ministry setting. If we carry out the process of mapping in the same old places where we do most of our thinking, we are less likely to break free into fresh perspectives. Find a library or a coffee shop where you've never been before. Take a little vacation somewhere if you can afford one. By manipulating your own space, you will help your mind acquire new perspectives on your church family system.

Second, it is always advantageous to do this with the help of a trusted colleague from outside one's own ministry setting. Such a person (or even a small group of such persons) can help us see things we otherwise would have missed because of our immersion in the situation. And they can do so just by asking questions.

The Narrative

1. Describe to yourself an event in the life of your congregation that illustrates a typical block to ministry or a recurring sort of conflict.

Put this event in narrative terms. What led up to it? Who was involved? What happened? Try to recall exactly what people said at key points. Be as objectively descriptive as possible. Don't assume that what you were feeling during the event is what everyone else was feeling or that how you interpreted the event at the time is the way others saw it. Pay attention to what people said and did, including what you can remember of their nonverbal actions. Use your observations to draw tentative conclusions about what they were thinking and how they were feeling.

For example, after telling the story about how young children began coming up into the choir loft to sing in the choir, Steve Adams commented, "Now that frustrated the choir." When asked to elaborate, he said, "They just sit there and they get upset, but they don't do anything about it." When asked how he knew they were upset, he reflected that maybe they weren't upset, at least not all of them.

The Players

2. Who are the principal players in the event?

Draw the outer markings of a parental boundary on a sheet of paper: |-   -|

Write in the names of the central players first. For example, let's imagine that you have told the story of a board meeting in which "Mildred blew up at Harry." Mildred and Harry go on the map first. At this point you must make a tentative judgment about whether to place one or both of them above or below the line. The best way to decide is to ask whether there are people in the congregation who defer to them. Do they have children? If you identify a subsystem of children, place Mildred and Harry above the parental boundary and the children below the boundary, labeling the children in a convenient way. You may want to interpret their identity or self-understanding by giving them a name of your own invention, such as "The We-Never-Let-the-Church-Down People."

3. What subsystems are involved in the conflict?

In identifying children for Mildred or Harry, you have identified a subsystem. But it's possible that each player's children form two or more subsystems. At this point one should make a tentative judgment about how important it is to represent this division. You may decide to draw circles as smaller subsystems within the larger circle representing all a player's children. Or you may decide that indicating the smaller subsystems is not relevant.

Showing the division of children into subsystems is important if (a) there is conflict between one or more of these subsystems or (b) one or more (but not all) of these subsystems are also children of another parent. Let's designate Harry as a parent affiliated with our imagined subsystem, The We-Never-Let-the-Church-Down People. We will make Mildred a parent for the Young Adults. Now we can map the relationships (see fig. 3).

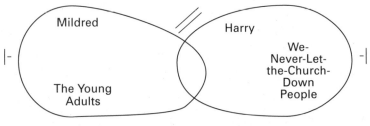

Figure 3

On this map we have indicated the conflict between Mildred and Harry, but we have not yet clarified the quality of the boundary between them. We have also drawn larger circles as a way of indicating which parents go with which children. The intersection of circles represents children common to both.

Before proceeding ask yourself one more time whether you have correctly identified the parents. Remember that Steve Adams overlooked Bill because Bill seemed undersocialized. He was also going to treat Laverne as a parent because she was a "mature adult." These are easy mistakes to make in mapping. The question is not, Who do I think deserves to be a parent? but, Who are the parents in fact?

4. *What affiliations are present?*

This question assumes that you have already put all the relevant parents and children on the map.

The question of affiliations asks you to identify who is emotionally linked to whom.[3] For example, parents and their children are typically affiliated. But affiliations are possible between any persons in the system.

In the conflict with John and Jane at Sable Valley Community Church (chapters 1 and 4), at least four significant subsystems came into play: John and Jane, the Deacon Board (an official subsystem), a group of Retirees, and a group of persons held in low repute (the Disreputables). The Retirees and the Disreputables had nothing to do with each other. But Pastor Peter Wells, in affiliation with the deacons, was also positively affiliated with both of these other groups.

In order to map the relationships of the subgroups at the time of the congregational meeting, we must place Peter and the deacons somewhere in the middle and locate the Retirees and the Disreputables on opposite sides of the map (see fig. 4). We should also explore the systemic family relationships between members of the Deacon Board and members of the other subsystems. The deacons, after all, are an official subgroup. Some may be parents, some parental children, others children. Perhaps some are children of parents among the Retirees. As it turns out, Chris Beuler, chair of the Deacon Board, is a "parental child" of Les Thompson, one of the Retirees. Peter ended up mapping Sable Valley Church as follows:

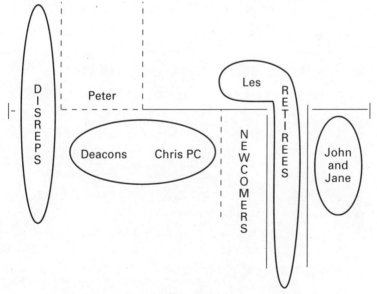

Figure 4

In order to discover what affiliations exist, it is helpful to ask questions such as, Who felt sorry for whom? or, With whom did so-and-so likely rehash the event after the meeting? or, Who likely supported whom in the gossip lines after the event? Another way to envision affiliations is to imagine that at the height of the conflict you could put all participants in a gymnasium and let them form groups as they wish.

5. *What coalitions formed?*

Who stood with whom? A coalition is an alliance, a taking of sides. Coalitions may form briefly between otherwise unaffiliated persons who discover common cause in the midst of a conflict. Or they may be the natural outgrowth of a long-term affiliation.

At Sable Valley the pastor and the deacons formed a coalition. But they failed to win the vote because the otherwise unaffiliated Retirees, Disreputables, and evidently some others formed a momentary coalition against them.

6. *Are there any ghosts?*

When it came time to elect new officers at Belleville Baptist, Bill wrote out a list of nominations and gave it to the chair of the nominating committee. Steve was taken aback. How had Bill come to decide that it was his job to guide the nominating process, much less to dictate who should be nominated? Steve tells a bit of history that suggests the answer to this question:

> *Steve:* Let me add something else. Bill exploded into these parenting roles after the former pastor left.
>
> *Hatfield:* He exploded into these roles?

Steve: I mean—that's my perception. Because the pastor had control of everything. Bill never went visiting with the former pastor and never—in every situation when there was conflict, the pastor won out over Bill.

So Bill has replaced Steve's predecessor. He assumed the pastoral function in the interim before Steve came, and to a large extent he still has the role. It turns out (as one might have guessed) that the former pastor, Arnold Aimes, used to compile a list of nominees and give it to the chair of the nominating committee. Bill, now the functioning parent-pastor, is simply following the former pastor's example.

In his retirement many miles away, Pastor Aimes is a living ghost in the Belleville Baptist family system. Pastor for twenty years, he still speaks with a grandfatherly voice, and it may be that Steve is the only person in the congregation who doesn't hear the voice of Aimes.

Label the ghosts on the map "grandparents" and put them in the appropriate place, above the whole church family or above subsystems over which they continue to have authority. You may want to place them in a "picture frame" to distinguish them from other family members.

7. Who is in charge of the family memory?

Often there is one or more persons serving as the family memory. Keepers of the family memory speak authoritatively about family history and about the opinions of the family ghosts. Their memory is often a largely fictitious reconstruction of the past. (After all, you can always bring the past back, even when it wasn't there to begin with!) But because the past usually carries weight with many family members, the keepers of the family memory have considerable power. Place them on the map. You can assume that they are parents. (Family memory is discussed further in chapter 7.)

8. *Where do you belong on the map?*

Pastors typically assume that they are parents, but often this is because they confuse their pastoral authority with their role in the family. In some traditions it is assumed that the pastoral role carries with it a parental identity within the church family system. In other traditions, it is not so assumed.

For example, Clayton Tinder (chapter 3) was clearly the father of his church. By contrast, Mark Rivers (chapter 1) possessed parental authority only within the confines of his office, which the Oakridge Presbyterian Church parents narrowly defined for their "foster child pastor."

There are forces working both for and against pastors who are assuming parental status in the church family. On one hand, the exercise of the pastoral office—through pastoral leadership and pastoral care—encourages members of the congregation to regard the pastor as a parent. On the other hand, congregations sometimes prefer to limit the pastor's authority to that of the pastoral office. Congregational family systems have a strong tendency to maintain homeostasis (the status quo). Pastors often want to change things. Therefore, congregational family systems sometimes perceive that they have a stake in keeping the pastor from assuming a parental role, especially a central one.

In locating yourself on the map it is important to be honest. You will not be able to formulate effective pastoral strategies if you aren't. For example, if you are an independent child in the congregation, but intend to implement strategies that only a parent can carry out, you are setting yourself up for frustration.

It may help you to place yourself more accurately if you ask yourself the following question. If I were to resign my pastoral office today but remain as a family member in the church, would I be a parent, a parental child, a child, or an independent child? In answering this question, think through your relationship with specific parents on your map.

The Family Boundaries

9. Can you sketch in some boundaries?

The basic parental boundary should already be in place on your map, although you should not yet have filled in its quality of communication. The task now is to determine that quality along its various segments. At this point you may want to review the three types of boundary quality discussed in chapter 2. Be certain not to assume that a close relationship must mean enmeshment or that conflict must signal a rigid boundary.

The map of Belleville (fig. 2) offers an example of how the parental boundary assumes different forms. The segment of the parental boundary between Bill and his children is rigid. The segment between the pastor and the congregational children is porous. And so forth.

Once you have filled in boundary quality along the parental boundary, go on to mark boundaries between other subsystems. Mark horizontal boundaries between parental children and the children under them. Use vertical boundary lines to indicate parity (nonparental) relations.[4] The map of Belleville (fig. 2), for example, shows vertical boundaries between Bill and the Newcomers, and between Margaret and Denise.

10. What do the boundaries on the map tell you at this point?

Analyze the boundaries. What do they say about the system? Do you find, for example, that two principal systems are walled off from each other? Are groups of children getting caught in a conflict between parents? Are parents fighting through children? Where are you in relation to the principal subsystems? Are you walled off from any key parents? Do you have conflict with any parents across a rigid boundary? Are your attempts to work personally on conflict in the church directed toward interaction with both children and parents or primarily with children—perhaps children of parents with whom you have conflict across a rigid boundary?

These questions do not by any means exhaust the possible learnings from reading a map. They do point to some typical insights to be gleaned from mapping. The examples also suggest two rules of thumb regarding communication and conflict within a system, especially if the system is a large one.

First, although healthy communication (a porous boundary) admits conflict, people generally throw up a wall if conflict persists, especially when nothing requires them to keep communicating. It is wise to assume that as conflict escalates rigid boundaries will be forming.

When this happens the most important thing to remember is that the problem is not the conflict but the rigid boundaries. Those who try to smooth over or repress conflict rather than let it come to the surface only add bricks to the walls that begin forming when conflict is present. Building rigid boundaries will not make the conflict go away. It will only suppress some of the immediate symptoms. Not only that, rigid boundaries make it more and more difficult for people to resolve the conflict and more and more likely that the conflict will erupt far more severely at some later point. In the meantime people will continue fighting without communicating directly. And these indirect fights will get in the way of ministry.

Second, when there is conflict across a rigid boundary between parents, they will typically carry out their indirect fight through third parties (triangulation), usually through children. And so the conflict grows. Where there are conflicted rigid boundaries between parents, look for indirect fighting through children.

It is very important that we apply these two rules of thumb not only to the group as a whole but also to our own patterns of interaction within the system. If I, an associate pastor, am in a conflicted relationship with Barbara, a key parent in the church, and a rigid boundary lies between us, then I won't feel inclined to speak directly and openly with her. I will want to avoid her. At a meeting where we are both present, I will choose a seat far away from her and will avoid making eye contact with her. If the conflict is severe, I may find it difficult even to turn my body in her direction. If we are sitting around a table or if I am leading the meeting, this may mean that I don't direct my face toward her part of the room. As a result, I end up symbolically walling off myself from the others who are sitting with her.

In an effort to deal with the conflict—perhaps at most just trying to protect myself and my interests politically—I may send messages to Barbara through other persons. Although I am unwilling to talk to her or even to some of the other parents allied with her, I may be willing to talk to some of her children. Perhaps I will try to smooth things over with Barbara through one of these children. Or maybe I'll try to win her children away from her. Probably I will carry out all such underground and indirect strategies without fully admitting to myself that I'm avoiding dealing with the conflict. After all, I'm probably acting the way just about everyone does when they're in my shoes. Perhaps the senior minister reinforces my behavior by accepting messages

about me from other people and delivering them to me
without insisting that those parties talk to me directly.

The Rules and Goals of the Game

Now we move to questions having to do with the dynamics and inner logic of the family system. We examine interactions between individuals but not on an individualistic level. We want to discover whether the conflict is governed by unspoken family rules and whether it is part of some hidden family game.

11. Ask people what the rules are.

This is a simple technique that is easy to overlook when faced with what appears to be a mystifying situation. "Are there any unspoken rules around here that I need to know about?" Insiders can usually tell you at least some of the rules, and they will usually divulge what they know unless a rule is embarrassing to them. You may find someone in the family who knows all the rules and likes to be frank, such as independent children who have been part of the family for a long time. Such people are sometimes treated as troublemakers because they keep mentioning what nobody's supposed to bring up at the dinner table. Make friends of these truth-tellers.

12. Listen for rules in everyday talk.

You can also identify hidden rules by listening to family talk for clues to family rules. When a member of the Searchers class (chapter 4) explained to Jerry that in order to teach "you have to be invited," that statement exposed a rule to any listener who had ears to hear and was looking for clues to family rules. In listening for rules, you should operate on the assumption that people implicitly know what the rules are and will express them, even if only indirectly and in seemingly inadvertent ways. Pay attention to everything, from the significant to the apparently trivial. And look for patterns in the explanations people offer for "how things are done around here."

13. Pay special attention when you do something that seems appropriate but you get in trouble for it. You have probably broken a rule.

Another way of discovering rules is by inadvertently breaking one. If you receive criticism for something that seems trivial to you, you have probably transgressed a family rule. Follow out the logic of the rule until you discover the game to which it belongs. Try to connect it with any other family rules you have identified.

Recall what happened when Pastor Stewart replaced the plastic flowers at the front of the sanctuary (chapter 4). He discovered that he'd broken an unspoken rule, which eventually became part of his hypothesis that he was in a family game called Death Watch.

14. What words are people using to describe what's going on? Do the words suggest a pattern?

Are people using metaphors that clue you in to what game they are playing? What metaphor would you use to describe the church or the conflict itself? What was it like? Write down a list of descriptive sentences. This church is like _____. This event was like _____. I feel like I'm _____. Ask others to offer descriptions of their experience of the focal event. Listen to the analogies and metaphors they use. Look especially for metaphors that come from family life. Once you have a leading metaphor, think it through systemically. Add detail to it from different people's points of view, as you discover these.

15. Do repeated outcomes suggest the existence of an unacknowledged family game?

To discern the presence of a game, one examines the outcomes of repeated behaviors and on that basis develops hunches of what people are trying to accomplish. This doesn't mean that people will be fully aware of the game they are playing. If the game is in some way shameful or embarrassing to them, they may be hiding the game not only from others but also from themselves. By testing what people say they want against the outcomes of their behavior (including what their communications do), we can hypothesize about the game they may be playing.

Tests of Whether Mapping Is Complete

Here are some questions that test whether you have finished mapping and are ready to begin building a strategy.

16. Do I have the big picture now, and do I understand how the different parts of the system relate? Apply this test to both the past and the future.

For example, looking back on events, do you now see where you are located in the family, what boundaries lie between you and others, and how your behaviors have been functioning in the system? Can you say, for instance, "Now I see why, when I do such-and-such, people don't respond as I expect"? Pastor Stewart might now say, "I see why, when I try to interest the church in a ministry to single adults or when I smile broadly and call for us all to be joyful in the Lord, my words don't touch any responsive chord. It's not that they don't have any energy;

it's that they're spending all their energy on a different game from the one I want to play."

Looking forward, can you make some plausible predictions of likely outcomes of an action taken by you or someone else in the system? For example, Peter Wells' map of Sable Valley (fig. 4) shows a rigid boundary between the Retirees and a group of Newcomers. He predicts that if he enlists some parents to help open up this boundary, the Retirees may lose interest in the game "Keep the Church the Same." He also predicts that if he concentrates on affirming the Disreputables and reassuring them of their secure place in the family, they will be less likely to continue supporting the rule that gives a free hand to John and Jane. Certainly he will never again lead his deacons to an all-church vote on John and Jane's membership unless he is certain that the church family, and not just the official systems, is prepared at least to censure John and Jane. But he also thinks it likely that if the Retirees quit playing the game "Keep the Church the Same" and if the Disreputables find acceptance, then John and Jane will lose their role in the family. What they would then do is anybody's guess. It's at least possible that the change in the system may change them. (Admittedly, it's more likely that they'll look for another congregation where they can play the game they want to play.)

Once you have worked your way through all the steps of mapping, examine the map to be certain that you have identified parents and children with accuracy and that you have marked the boundaries correctly. Be certain that you have not drawn in boundaries and located family members based only on your feelings. Reapply the defining charac-teristics of each of the mapping categories as objectively as you can to each person, subsystem, and boundary on the map. As a further check, ask yourself whether you have made any of the following easy mistakes: identifying some-one as a parent simply on the basis of his or her office or emotional maturity; concluding that a boundary is rigid because there is conflict across it; or assuming that there is enmeshment simply because two persons are very close.

After you have completed your map and rechecked it, you should spend some time monitoring family communi-cations to see whether your map rings true. Now that you have a basic grasp of the systems categories, you will be better able to interpret future interactions within the family as clues to family roles and boundaries.

In gathering information for mapping and in testing the accuracy of a map, it is extremely useful to keep a journal of family interactions, including narratives of "what happened" as well as brief verbatims of how conversations or discussions unfolded. Once you have objectified a set of conversations on paper, you can go back over them at your leisure and analyze the quality of communication that they reflect (see chapter 7). Taking time to revise your initial map after tracking family interactions will help ensure that the map on which you base your strategies accurately reflects the family structure.

Mapping Is Not Enough

A map is a tool that helps us acquire an understanding of the family system and to organize that understanding in a convenient form. But the reality of the congregation is always more complex and greater than our maps. By keeping in mind that a map is only one way of looking at the church, you will probably avoid using its symbols as pigeonholes, as if you had sufficiently comprehended individuals or groups of people as human beings and children of God merely by defining them as "parents" or "independent children."

Chapter Six

❖

Changing the Hidden System:

Focused Strategies

Sometimes Steve Adams feels like resigning his pastorate at Belleville. The problem with the choir is just one example of seemingly endless frustrations for him. From Steve's point of view, people have a minimum level of commitment and are content to let things remain the way they are. A few people have quit the choir. They may come back, but the choir holds to its old familiar patterns. Things are the same with the church as a whole. The congregation seems at the same time both stubborn and lethargic.

Because Steve is out of energy, he assumes that others feel the same way. The fact that he can't persuade the church to change in even modest ways convinces him that the church itself has as little energy as he does. Everybody's tired. He imagines that if things are going to improve, he'll have to muster more energy and infuse the system with power. He hopes that if he gives more of himself, God will pour the Spirit into the church and revive it from its stupor.

This is a very natural but also a very wrongheaded way to think. The pastor is not responsible for supplying the family system with the energy needed to make it function effectively. Not only is the attempt to do so a sure path to pastoral burn-out, it also doesn't honor the responsibility of the congregational system for itself. Nor is there any theological reason to assume that God will withhold the Spirit until Steve tries harder.

In fact, this impossible task of pumping energy into the system isn't necessary. As a family system the congregation already possesses the natural powers to sustain its own life and to adapt to changing circumstances. If the system appears lethargic, empty of human spirit, this does not mean that it's out of energy. It probably means that the energy of the system is being used in enormous amounts to maintain homeostasis: to keep things the same.

A systems approach to congregational life assumes that the human powers for preservation, healing, and change are already resident in the congregation. We understand these human powers as God-given, and we assume that God's Spirit is needed to guide and strengthen whatever natural strength the family system may already possess as a social system. But our focus here is not on the relationship of the Spirit to the church, much less on how one might devise techniques or offer prayers to garner the Spirit's power. Our focus is the natural human powers of the church family and how a systems approach can help one direct these human energies in ways that will promote the church's maturation as God's family. The remaining chapters present strategies for doing so.

Four Axioms

Four axioms provide the basis for a family systems approach to restructuring a conflicted congregational family:[1]

First, the congregational system is interconnected. This means that a consistent change in behavior by one family member will evoke change elsewhere in the system. The degree of change will depend on the role of that member in the system and the extent to which boundaries are kept open. But opening up boundaries is itself a primary way to evoke systemic change.

Second, the congregational system is both dynamic and stable. Even though family systems tend toward homeostasis (keeping themselves the same), they can also adapt to pressure from changes within or outside the system by restructuring themselves. While the family tendency toward homeostasis acts as a constraint on change, it also serves to preserve healthful changes once they have been made. And one result of any change in family structure is new possibilities for future change. One never runs out of possible strategies.

Third, the congregational family is already organized to care for its own members. The pastoral task is not to nurture the family singlehandedly but to help modify and strengthen the family system so that the family itself can better support and care for its members. This includes teaching parents how to nurture, fostering good communication to keep boundaries open, and encouraging nurturance as the primary style of authority in the family.

Fourth, the psychic life of the individual is not only private ("internal") but also social. Individuals influence and are influenced by the environment (system) in which they find themselves. If the system changes, they feel and act differently. This axiom means that we can approach the individual through the system and at the same time affect the system through the individual. When addressing church conflict, the pastor is always working in both ways. But one can waste a great deal of time and energy trying to change a system through individuals apart from any clear understanding of the role of those individuals in the family system. Mapping (chapter 5) provides information about the system as a basis for strategic approaches to conflict and long-term family restructuring.

These strategic approaches aim at mobilizing the indigenous parents and powers already resident in the system (axiom three). Pastors help restructure the family system by their own strategic participation in it.

Strategic Participation

Therapists use the clinical term *intervention* to describe the help given by the family therapist to the family. "Intervention" suggests an action from outside, and the therapist is in fact an outsider who joins the family only temporarily. Yet it is fundamental to Minuchin's approach that the therapist function as part of the system. To this extent, the therapist's interventions are insider action, what we might term strategic participation in the system. "Strategic participation" is an especially fitting way to describe a ministerial role in the congregational family system. Although pastors sometimes remain outsiders because they never do join the church family, those who do join are in a position to practice strategic insider action as family members. In fact, "joining" is itself a strategic action.

The therapeutic term *intervention* also suggests that there are "techniques" for making good families just as there are techniques for making good cars. Family therapists speak of techniques, but they also poke fun at their own tendency to imagine that they've discovered "The Technique."[2] There are elements of creativity and unpredictability in human beings that make it impossible to predict human behavior with scientific precision. And what you cannot predict, you cannot control with technique. So the pastor, like the therapist, must remain flexible and creative.

Fortunately, human systems do exhibit regular tendencies. And we have spent several chapters laying down the forms and logic of these tendencies for the local church family. Hunches based on a map of the congregational system are informed ways of imagining what will happen if one undertakes this or that strategy.

One thing that will always happen is that the system will adjust in some way to what we do. The church family is always undergoing self-adjustments. The map keeps changing— sometimes in little ways, sometimes in big ones. And that means that with every strategic step, new possibilities arise.

Focusing

The core of a systemic approach is the focused strategy. All ministry must be selective in order to be effective. Even a small congregation presents both too many opportunities and too many problems for ministry. The minister is therefore often compelled to focus on what appear to be the most pressing problems. But appearances can be deceiving. Perhaps what is apparently most pressing is not the most significant problem. The tyranny of the urgent can prevent a pastor from getting to more fundamental, underlying issues, for which the problem of the moment is only one symptom. A systemic strategy brings together the demands of the urgent and the goal of working on deeper, underlying issues to achieve long-term growth. It lets one work at the same time on both the problem at hand (the known and immediate conflict) and whatever underlying issues there may be.

By mapping the family system through focus on a recurrent area of conflict or blockage to ministry, the pastor is able to identify certain critical structural points in the system. On the basis of this mapping, the pastor then devises a plan for modifying the system. This is the focused strategy, and it will include a number of maneuvers. The map itself is already a focus, because it portrays the system from the standpoint of a particular event (or cluster of events), in which certain participants come into the foreground, while others remain in the background. The map reveals all sorts of possibilities for action. Out of this range of possibilities, the pastor focuses energy strategically on selected points in the system. Usually a number of strategies suggest themselves. It is rarely a question of finding the one right thing that will work. And if one strategy fails, there are always more to be tried.

But while carrying out focused strategies, the pastor can also participate strategically in the family system in routine ways. At every point in the life of the family, the pastor can monitor the communication patterns (which determine the nature and quality of boundaries in the family system) and work to foster and maintain clear and open boundaries throughout the system. Focused strategies provide an immediate way to deal with church conflict. But by practicing focused strategies one is already building up a repertoire of skills for routine "preventive medicine" in caring for the church family system.

There are two mistakes that pastors are most prone to make in devising strategies on the basis of their maps. The first is to think in individualistic rather than systemic ways. If your proposed strategies are predominantly efforts where you work one-on-one with individual family members, then you are not yet thinking and strategizing systemically. Your strategies ought to involve enlisting parents to help restructure the family. And while some pastoral nurturing of individuals (especially key parents and potential parents) is often essential, systemic strategies must involve work with subsystems as a whole, large and small.

The second mistake is to strategize for political victory and not for the sake of all family members. If you use your map to devise power plays aimed only at helping you to win some particular battle in the church, then you are not nurturing the system. Remember that every set of strategies either reinforces existing family rules or establishes new precedents, which may in turn become established family rules. The family process that your strategies support ought to honor the voices of all family members and teach by example how the family can work out differences fairly. Even those who "deserve to lose" by your estimation, deserve nonetheless to be treated fairly in the process itself. If they aren't, your strategic process is only reinforcing the common human rationalization that says, "Because we know we're right, and those others have been doing wrong, we are justified in treating them the way they've treated us." This does not mean that your strategies should be designed to ensure at all costs that no one resigns a position or leaves the church. Your strategies should be designed so that if persons make such decisions, they do so for reasons other than that they were mistreated.

Keeping Boundaries Open

Many of the strategies we propose are efforts to modify nonporous boundaries so that conflict comes out into the open where the family can deal with it fairly and constructively. But handling conflict openly often does not last very long because people find it easier psychologically to mask the real issues, to fight through third parties, to shut down communication when things get too heated, and so on. Boundaries may open up in the midst of a conflict only to close down all over again because people cannot tolerate the tension of an open fight. If open disagreement over the real issues feels too painful, people will resort to underground and indirect forms of conflict, all of which encourage rigid boundaries to form all over again.

Therefore it is very important to provide incentives for keeping the boundaries open. The basic strategy for accomplishing this is affiliation.

Affiliation

Remember Pastor Jim Roper and his conflicts with Ellis Campbell and Harriet Walters? They said that his preaching was too negative, and they had lots of other advice for him about how he should change his pastoral style. They were also at the center of conflicts he was having with the congregation as a whole over his ministry style. Harriet sought to control Jim through maternalistic forms of manipulation. Jim resisted by adopting an autonomistic style of authority in response. Harriet countered by starting a campaign behind the scenes to pressure Jim to resign, enlisting Ellis in the effort.

Mapping revealed to Jim that in approaching his conflicts with the church family over his ministry style, he was concentrating his efforts in some wrong places. He was faithfully working on his relationship with Ellis: making it a point to talk to Ellis each Sunday, having regular lunches with him, and so on. He was doing all this on the assumption that a good relationship with Ellis would (1) have positive effects on the conflicts between him and others in the congregation (such as Harriet) and (2) also lessen conflicts between the younger leaders aligned with himself and the older leaders aligned with Ellis. But Ellis was a parental child, who took his cues from Harriet. Since Jim was practically avoiding Harriet, one of the most powerful parents in the church, all his efforts with Ellis did little more than create good feelings between the two of them over a lunch hour.

An autonomistic style affords Jim some psychological breathing room with Harriet, but it doesn't work as a style of authority, because autonomism assumes that one is already recognized as a parent. But Harriet, although she honors Jim's pastoral role and prerogatives, doesn't recognize him as a parent. The boundary between them is in fact disputed. Harriet, in her maternalistic style, in effect views Jim as a child ("below the line") or at least as someone who ought to assume a child role with her. But Jim sees their relationship as one of parental parity. (Keep in mind that Jim is not in a dependent or "co-dependent" relationship with Harriet. His problem is not how to resist her efforts to influence him but how to resist his own inclinations to have nothing to do with her.) Using the autonomistic style with Harriet doesn't help Jim work out conflicts in the church family. It only makes matters worse. It creates increasing affiliation distance between Jim and Harriet, which makes Harriet more and more unhappy with Jim. And because she is an influential mother in the church family, her conflicts with Jim radiate through the church as a whole. Both Harriet's and Jim's congregational children get drawn into the conflict.

After mapping his church family, Jim decided to affiliate with Harriet. To affiliate is to lessen the distance on either side of a boundary between oneself and another person.

Affiliation means identifying oneself positively with a sub-system, whether a person or a group. It requires sufficient investment of time and energy to build some sense of mutual identity and closeness.

In the large and complex congregational family system, much more so than in the small confines of the literal family, it is impracticeable for the pastor to give equal attention to every person and subsystem. Pastors are always making—or are being pressured into making—selective allocations of their time and emotions. Affiliation is a strategic way of being responsibly selective.

There are three basic and mutually reinforcing ways to affiliate: affirmation, sympathy, and identification.

Affirmation means finding things to value in the other and expressing appreciation and praise for those things. In affiliating one attends to what is positive rather than to what is negative in the other.

Sympathy means responding with understanding to the other's emotional expressions of anger, depression, frustration, tiredness, and so forth. Like affirmation, sympathy requires attending to what we find understandable rather than focusing on what we think is unjustified or unreasonable.

Identification means discovering and matching similarities between ourselves and others. We express ways in which we are alike, how we have (or have had) similar feelings, ideas, experiences. Since we are in fact all both similar and different from one another, identification means highlighting what is the same about us.

Jim decided that affiliation with Harriet would work for him only if he carried it out in a controlled environment. Since the church had just added an associate pastor, Jim took this as an occasion to foster church staff identity through regular weekly staff meetings comprising him, the new pastor, and Harriet as minister of music. These meetings gave Harriet regular access to him, and it also provided a framework in which he could affirm her work. Being included by the two pastors in an inner circle of three also helped her know that her participation in decision making mattered to them and that they esteemed her ministry.

Jim used an organizational adjustment as an occasion to change his family relationship to Harriet. The effects of the family change began to radiate through other parts of the family system. In time Jim noticed the conflicts beginning to ease between him and Harriet (and her co-parents and children, including Ellis). Jim and Harriet could now work through ordinary conflicts without crisis. In the ensuing months, neither Ellis nor Harriet carried out any campaigns against Jim. Not only that, other parents, younger persons whom Jim had nurtured for leadership roles, began receiving greater parental recognition throughout the church family.

We have just examined a technique of pastoral affiliation with a church parent. But it is just as important to help parents affiliate with one another. Fostering affiliation among church parents is a significant part of any strategy to open up rigid boundaries between them. There are many ways to go about this. In what follows, we offer two basic strategies for fostering affiliation: manipulating space and making use of family play. These are meant only to be exemplary and not exhaustive of the approaches one can take to creating strategic affiliations. What is important is to be guided by your map of the family. Use the map to identify the boundaries in the system where you need to concentrate your imagination and energies.

Manipulating Space

At Parkside Presbyterian Church, a "Dream Committee" had just been constituted to envision some new ministry futures for the church. Evelyn, a congregational parent in one influential subsystem, and Frank, a parent from another influential subsystem, were both on this committee, and from the beginning they opposed each other's ideas. Their uncompromising positions against each other soon began to impede the work of the committee, and pastor Tony Matera was uncertain what he could do about it.

Tony suspected that Evelyn and Frank were not just battling about the ideas on the table but were fighting out a long-standing tension between the two subsystems they represented. But this only made matters more delicate for him. He didn't want to get caught in the middle of a fight between these two powerful parents and the subsystems they represented. It seemed to him that the best way for him to both look and be neutral was to do nothing at all.

One evening the committee experienced a breakthrough on a critical aspect of its agenda. It happened, Tony later reported, when "Frank turned to Evelyn, who was sitting next to him, and said, 'I think I can go along with you on that.' " Did the two usually sit next to each other at meetings? No, they would typically sit far apart. But that evening Frank arrived to the meeting late and found that the only available seat was next to Evelyn.

Tony learned a very important lesson of communication from this event. Spatial proximity can influence boundaries; hence, the manipulation of space is one way of working on boundaries. An accident of seating had forced Evelyn and Frank into a spatial affiliation that served almost immediately as a basis for one to listen to the other and bend in the other's direction toward compromise.

Space is a metaphor for affiliation. We say that people are "close," that someone seems "distant," or that people need to "work together." Manipulating literal space to put people into proximity also influences them to move toward emotional affiliation. And emotional affiliation is an incentive to keep a boundary open.

Play

Affiliation comes through life together. In the church family it is formed in many ways, one of the most important of which is play. When people are together (spatial proximity) and are encouraged to play, they form affiliations.

Pastor Louise Kennedy invites people to play in all sorts of church settings. She does this by introducing the verbal play of humor into various settings, from sermons to business meetings. Her use of humor is not just a good way to communicate with people, it also helps people affiliate with one another. Louise's humor also encourages others to engage in verbal play. Family talk at her church is always seasoned with a bit of comedy—sometimes to release tension, sometimes just for the fun of it. And this use of humor becomes a tie that binds.

Weaving humor through the life of the church family is a strategy for nurturing affiliations. Conflict can feel like very sober business. If the family fights too earnestly and humorlessly, any boundaries that the pastor or others help to open up are likely to become rigid again very quickly. Shared laughter creates and reinforces affiliation. Affiliation provides an emotional incentive for family members to work at opening up boundaries and keeping them open.

It not only releases tension in the midst of a conflict, it also sustains family structures that make conflict resolution possible.

Besides humor, there are many other forms of play that church families typically structure into their life together, from all-church picnics to the recreational activities of various subsystems. The pastor, with the help of other family members, can use such events (and invent others) as occasions to foster strategic affiliations within the congregation. The pastor can bring together unaffiliated parents in play. By putting unaffiliated parents into partnerships of play (games, skits, etc.), pastors help create the conditions under which affiliations can form.

It is very important to work simultaneously at affiliation and modifying boundaries, since they reinforce each other in critical ways. The naive pastor imagines that communication will get better and conflict will go away just because people affiliate by learning to laugh and play together. The pastor who thinks that teaching, reinforcing, modeling, and nurturing in order to improve communication are enough to foster open boundaries so that conflicts can be resolved is probably going to be disappointed. A double strategy is needed. Unless parents are affiliated, conflicted boundaries between them are unlikely to open up and remain open. But affiliation itself does not determine boundary quality. Therefore, it is important to work on boundary quality (see the strategies in chapter 7) at the same time one works on fostering affiliation. Play provides an enjoyable and nonthreatening framework in which to do both.

Unbalancing Tactics

Whenever a system is experiencing disequilibrium, possibilities for restructuring are present. A change of pastors creates disequilibrium, sometimes of an extreme form. But disequilibrium occurs in the church family for many other reasons. Although it produces discomfort, disequilibrium should be viewed as an opportunity for healthful change. And when the system needs restructuring but is experiencing no disequilibrium, the thing to do is unbalance it.

The basic destabilizing tactic in structural family systems theory is coalition. Coalitions form naturally in family systems, with helpful or hurtful results. One way to counteract a hurtful coalition of a strong subsystem against a weaker one is to take the weaker one's side.

As a pastoral strategy, the aim of such a coalition is to unbalance the system so that it can restructure itself in a way that eliminates the warfare between the two subsystems. If coalition is likely only to produce an increased polarization, then it will not unbalance the system. Therefore the pastor who enters into a coalition in order to destabilize the system must be affiliated already with parents throughout the system. Otherwise the coalition will not destabilize but only polarize. The pastor must also be a parent in the family system, because only those with parental authority in the system can use coalition constructively as an unbalancing technique.

Coalition contributes more power to those with whom one aligns and is therefore especially appropriate with weaker members in the system. There are only two circumstances that justify entering into a coalition with powerful parents. First, such a coalition is warranted when an ethical issue is at stake on which one has to take a stand. Second, a coalition with powerful parents is justified when it is carried out in an exaggerated way, as a kind of parody, in order to make overbearing parents confront the way in which they themselves use their authority. But one must be sure they get the point.

Coalition as an unbalancing technique is a promising approach to the conflict in the Searchers class over Jerry, the unwelcome member (chapter 4). Imagine two leading class parents (Art and Pam) carrying out such a strategy. They begin by affiliating with Jerry. They go out of their way to talk to him each Sunday before class, and they make it a habit to sit with him, one on either side (manipulation of space).

The next stage of this scenario is the coalition itself. Art and Pam align themselves with Jerry by affirming his contributions in class and by publicly taking his side, as often as they can, in class disagreements. Whatever Jerry says, they focus on some positive aspect of it with which they agree. This maneuver will unbalance the system, and it offers a good chance for moving the group to acknowledge Jerry's full right to membership. The system will seek equilibrium, and with Art and Pam on Jerry's side, one way for the system to stabilize itself is for its other members to affiliate with Jerry. Less likely is that the system will become polarized, so that Art and Pam lose their status as parents and become marginalized with Jerry. Alienating Art and Pam is too costly emotionally and probably "politically" too complex. The system is likely to seek the simple path of least resistance.

Pam and Art can smooth that path by being careful how they express themselves in "taking sides" with Jerry. If they do so in ways that are antagonistic toward others, they will prolong the period of destabilization. If they align themselves with Jerry gracefully, affirming others in the process, the system will restructure more quickly to affiliate with Jerry.

This strategy has a good chance of resolving the class tension focused on Jerry. But it may not lead to an exposure of the rule, "You have to be invited." In order to challenge the rule, supplemental strategies are required. For example, Pam and Art might propose that the class place an announcement in the church bulletin and newsletter inviting anyone to join them for their next study series. If there is resistance from the class to this suggestion, then Pam and Art can press the class to consider whether it is operating with an exclusivistic invitation rule. They might go on to urge the class to adopt the theme of Christian acceptance and inclusiveness as a study focus.

Marking Boundaries

Marking boundaries is a third basic pastoral strategy for restructuring the system so that the church family can handle conflict constructively.

We begin by looking at some examples of everyday boundary marking in the church family. Then we show how marking boundaries can serve as a strategy in a church conflict. Since boundary marking is a point of intersection between official and familial systems, we examine official and familial boundary marking and show how they can be interrelated.

The first week of Larry Daniels' ministry at Fairfax United Methodist Church, a film was shown on a Sunday evening during an all-church event. The next morning the pastor found on his desk a gray box containing the reel of film. With it was a note: "Pastor this film needs to be returned to _____. Thanks." The note was signed by Tim Arnold, a member of the worship committee that had planned the Sunday evening event. Larry returned the film and dropped Tim a note, thanking him for his work on the worship committee. But at the end of the note Larry added a P.S., which said: "By the way, it was good that I came into the office this morning and wasn't visiting someone in the hospital, otherwise I wouldn't have discovered the film you left on my desk. Next time, please check out first whether I will be able to do you the favor of returning a film, or whatever it may be." With this note Larry began to mark a boundary between himself as pastor and parishioner Tim as a worship committee member. He clarified the nature of the official boundary between them by saying, in effect, "It is not my job as pastor to do errands for church committees." He was also straightforward in communicating with Tim, exercising a style of interaction that will help keep this boundary porous.

Several weeks later Larry was hanging wallpaper in his kitchen at the parsonage, when Janet and Bruce Jenkins stopped by. The following conversation took place:

Bruce: Is that straight, Larry?

Larry: Yes, it's straight.

Bruce: How do you know it's straight?

Larry: Well, I used a plumb line and a level.

Bruce: Oh, but it doesn't look straight.

Larry: Well, it is straight.

Bruce: (after a pause) We couldn't live in a house where the wallpaper wasn't straight enough.

Larry: (laughing) Well, we live here and this really appears straight enough to us.

Bruce: Would you like to come to our house sometime and look at our wallpaper?

Larry: You know, we'd be happy to come and see how your house is decorated, and I'm sure it's very tastefully done.

At this point Bruce volunteered to take over.

Bruce comes with boundary-marking invitations of an informal, familial sort. The first invitation is for Larry to accept the role of teachable child: "I'll show you how to do that, so you can get it right." The second invitation is for Larry to be a helpless child: "Here, let me do that for you." Larry responds with boundary-marking moves of his own, refusing at each point to accept the invitations to play child.

Interactions of this sort happen constantly in human life, and they are especially formative at the beginning of a human relationship. In the local congregation, exchanges between people over little things create patterns of leadership and deferral which prepare the ground for the establishment of parents and children in church family decision-making processes.

Let's look at another example. Imagine Larry inviting Sheryl Anderson to work with Bruce in planning a series of monthly Sunday evening "forums" on issues of family and society. Bruce comes to the first meeting with an outline of topics and a detailed description of the format. Sheryl hasn't thought to prepare anything in writing because she assumed they would begin by "brainstorming" together. Bruce introduces the material he has prepared by saying, "I thought we could do something like this; we'll have . . ." Between "we could" and "we'll have," Sheryl senses that influence in the decision-making process is already slipping away from her.

To offset Bruce's one-sided control, Sheryl begins asking friendly questions, hoping he'll see that his proposal is only one of any number of possible ways to proceed. Bruce becomes defensive and belittles her comments, then "excuses" her by suggesting that she probably hasn't had very much experience at this sort of thing. Sheryl tells him that her idea of planning is that they would discuss different ideas together until they had a variety of possible options and then they would work together in making choices toward a common plan. Bruce says he doesn't have time for that kind of drawn-out planning. That's what he hates about church committees. The conversation continues as follows:

Bruce: People just talk in circles and at the end everyone's tired and nothing's decided. I only agreed to do this because it would just be two of us and we could work efficiently.

Sheryl: But we have to work together.

Bruce: O.K., right, so I went to a lot of work to make up the format and think up some topics that would go together in a logical order. I was hoping you could call some of these people *(points to a list)* who might be speakers.

Sheryl: Bruce, I'm not the secretary for our planning team. Let's go back to the beginning. Let's take a blank sheet of paper and start listing some possible topics and ways to structure the forums. We'll put your ideas down. You have some good ones. But let's come up with more before we settle on a single plan.

Bruce gives Sheryl invitation after invitation to assume the role of child. She refuses them all and thus marks a parity boundary between herself and Bruce.

But suppose it had been not Sheryl but July Fischer who'd been asked to work with Bruce. Unlike Sheryl, July has little confidence in herself and her own ideas. Once Bruce pulls out his papers and begins talking, she accepts the role of child and quickly regrets ever having agreed to be one of the planners (since "I never have anything to contribute"). She overestimates the quality of Bruce's ideas and feels intimidated as a result. Suppose, further, that Bruce treats July in a gently patronizing way. She ends up admiring him. Instead of marking a parity boundary, she has cooperated in marking a parental boundary, and has taken a first step toward becoming one of Bruce's congregational children. In the next chapter we will discuss ways in which July's pastor, Larry, can practice strategic church family nurture in a way that supports July toward greater independence.

Sometimes two levels of boundary marking—one official and the other informal—are happening at once. In the exchange between Tim and Larry over the film, there was also an informal, familial dimension. "Tim wanted desperately to please me and be buddies with me," Larry explains. From Tim's standpoint, leaving the film with the note was an invitation to chummy brotherliness. Tim presumed a degree of friendship that implied, in Larry's words, "We can expect the other one to do things for us without clearing it." Larry wasn't ready for this degree of friendship (after being in town only a week!), so he marked the family (sibling) boundary between them at a different point of distance from what Tim wanted. The note he sent to Tim, signed informally "Larry" but referring to his pastoral role and responsibilities, sent boundary-marking messages at two levels. In marking the official boundary (first level) Larry also indicated that, at least for the time being, there needed to be more affiliation distance on either side of the family boundary between them (second level).

Having offered some isolated examples of official and familial boundary marking, we now turn to discuss boundary marking as a strategy in the midst of a church conflict.

Childlife at Lincoln Baptist

In the last year of his pastorate, pastor Ed Stone lost his wife to cancer. Her death no doubt contributed to his decision to take an early retirement. Loren Rivers was Ed's associate, and the church invited Loren to assume the senior pastoral role. Loren accepted. It is now October, three months into Loren's pastorate, and he is facing his first acute church conflict. It concerns the Lincoln Baptist Childlife Center.

The Childlife Center is a day-care service run by the church as a way of providing low-cost child care for families in the church and in the wider community. The Center is governed by a church board, which hires the director for the Center. The director in turn secures a staff. Although the Center charges for its services, it is heavily subsidized by the church.

Rising costs, low enrollment of children in the Center, and a tightening church budget have precipitated a crisis. Loren is trying to get caught up on the details as conflicts in the Childlife Board begin to erupt and radiate throughout the church.

Loren learns that the previous spring, when it was time to renew the contracts for the director and the staff, the Childlife Board was doubtful that the church could afford to continue operating the Childlife Center. But the contracts were renewed and no action was taken to curb expenses. Now in October, after the summer school break, the Center has resumed its services, but the Board is talking even more seriously about closing the Center or cutting its budget. Anne Lawrence, director of Childlife Center, maintains that the church is obligated to meet its commitments to the Center for that year (fall to spring). The Childlife Board is divided about what to do, and a significant number of people in the church are up in arms about the problem.

Loren is confused about why the Childlife Board didn't act last spring, and he doesn't understand why the Board is now simply letting the conflict mount. In order to view the problem in systemic terms, he sketches a map that depicts the official systems familially.

Mapping the official systems reveals a structural pattern in the way all the church boards function (fig. 1). Former pastor Ed previously attended all church board meetings and dominated them. When Loren asks himself where the various church boards belong on the map, he realizes that during Ed's pastorate they were all below the parental boundary. It seems logical to assume that the boards are still functioning below the line. That would explain the immobility of the Childlife Board.

The Ghost of Pastor Ed Stone
[Pastor Loren?]

PC Trustees	PC Deacon Board	PC Childlife Board	PC Mission Board	PC (other boards)	PC Advisory Council (composed of board chairs)

Figure 1

The boards are all in the role of parental children, accustomed to deferring to pastor-parent Ed in making decisions. But Loren hasn't accepted this traditional pastoral role. He prefers a nonpaternalistic pastoral style, one that limits pastoral authority and puts him in partnership with other officers and official structures. In other words, he imagines the official system as follows (fig. 2):

Figure 2

Loren's picture of the official systems is technically correct but does not accurately reflect how the boards actually function. The two maps (figs. 1 and 2) show that the congregation and the pastor are operating with conflicting conceptions of the official system and its structures of authority. When Loren refuses to attend all board meetings, the church wonders why the new pastor is not functioning like a parent, and the new pastor wonders why the boards are not functioning like boards.

Now let's look at the unofficial family system. As Loren later reflected on it, none of the persons on the boards is a parent in the church family system! The congregational family encourages parental children in the system to seek (or at least accept) office, while the parents, who tend to be constellated in an older generation, function as grandparents. During Ed's pastoral tenure, the Grandparents gave over parental authority to the pastor, who served as the single parent in the family system. The former pastor accepted this role, and his paternalistic leadership style encouraged the church officers to remain parental children. Under this arrangement, church officers would carry out responsibility and exercise authority in the system only with the permission and guidance of the pastor parent, who was ever present. As a result, the boards began to function as parental children. The official structure became functionally subordinated to the familial structure, with the pastor serving as chief parent in both systems.

The Grandparents in this family possess real authority over the family as a whole. They can make or break the pastor. But as long as the pastor does an acceptable job of parenting, they don't intervene.

Grieving over the loss of his wife, Ed participated in church life less and less during the last months of his pastorate. He quit attending most board meetings and for the most part gave up his parental role. This threw the church family system into disequilibrium. A parental vacuum formed and the congregation became crippled under stress. The new pastor has refused to assume the role of single parent, creating even more disequilibrium in the system.

The following map (fig. 3) superimposes the familial structure onto the official structure. We have used the designation "PC" to indicate parental children in the family

The Grandparents

The Ghost of Pastor Stone

Pastor Loren Rivers?

OPC Trustees made up of PC's	OPC Deacon Board made up of PC's	OPC Childlife Board made up of PC's	OPC Mission Board made up of PC's	OPC other boards, made up of PC's	OPC Advisory Council made up of PC's

The Rest of the Children

Congregational Members, Childlife Employees

Figure 3

system and the designation "OPC" to indicate the boards as "official" parental children.

Systems seek homeostasis. In this case the parental children are pressuring Loren to take matters in hand (the way the former pastor always did), and the Grandparents are getting ready to intervene. From the Grandparents' point of view, the new pastor must prove that he can handle the children, or else his tenure as pastor will be short-lived.

The most pressing task for Loren is to clarify the nature of the boundary between himself and the parental children. Given the fact that the familial structure governs the official structure, this means that Loren must either accept the traditional role of single paternalistic parent or change the system by redefining his role. Since assuming the senior pastoral office, Loren has been trying to redefine the pastoral role within the church. In accepting the pastoral call, he had made it clear that he would not attend all board meetings. And on those occasions when he has met with boards, he has assumed a posture of collegiality and shared authority.

What Loren did not recognize was that the church system would be thrown into disequilibrium by his pastoral style. Given the nature of the reigning familial structure, the church was more apt to seek homeostasis than to change. Had the boards included parents who resented the former pastor's encroachment on their parental authority, they would likely have welcomed Loren's pastoral style. But boards made up of parental children are not going to move across the parental boundary to function as collegial executives overnight.

In the light of what he learned from mapping, Loren decided that the only workable strategy was to accept enough of the traditional role of single parent to allow the system to reach a measure of functioning homeostasis. In short, Loren concluded that one element of his focused strategy would be to clarify the boundary between himself and the boards by re-marking the old boundary.

The decision to re-mark the old boundary did not mean that Loren would have to function across this boundary in the paternalistic manner of Ed. Instead Loren determined to begin nurturing the parental children to become full-fledged parents.

Once Loren began to mark the old parental boundary by attending board meetings and exercising more executive leadership, the Grandparents breathed a sigh of relief. Loren gained their confidence. And if he keeps building their confidence in him, he has the hope of enlisting them in the work of restructuring the system so that it fosters growth in its children instead of stifling them.

What lies in the future for Loren and Lincoln Baptist? If the parental children become parents and the boards assume independent parental roles, the church will face a new problem: how decision making can take place at an official level if all the boards have an independent and equal status. In the present structure the only coordination between boards is through the Advisory Council. But this council has no authority over the various boards. It can only gather information from the boards and offer advice. If there is a conflict in an area where more than one board has authority (e.g., the Childlife Center Board works up a budget that the Finance Committee rejects) there is no way to adjudicate the conflict efficiently and fairly at an official level.

In the days when Ed had unquestioned parental say in all the boards, he could resolve any such conflicts single-handedly (or prevent them from even emerging). With his departure and Loren's refusal to operate in a paternalistic style, the official system is moving toward a crisis of authority. As the boards "grow up" and Loren is able to relinquish more and more authority over them, conflicts between the boards are inevitable. A structural solution is to establish an executive board in place of the Advisory Council and invest it with final decision-making authority in adjudicating matters between the boards. Loren begins to promote the idea of establishing an executive council at the same time that he works to nurture parental children toward more independent functioning.

Long-term and Short-term

Most of the strategies we have described thus far involve both immediate measures in the midst of a conflict and long-term approaches to restructuring the church family system. Out of systemic responses to crises the wise pastor devises continuing strategies for nurturing the system. As one can gather from the strategies we have already introduced, nurture is central to long-term systemic care for the church family. And at the heart of continuing nurture is the task of training family members in good communication.

Next we discuss regulating and modeling good communication in the church family system. This will provide further guidance for monitoring and modifying communication patterns as part of focused strategies. It will also furnish additional direction in how to carry out continuing nurturance as a routine strategy of pastoral care for the church family system.

Chapter Seven

❖

Spreading the Blue Chips:

Communication and Power

Communication is a currency of power. Consider something as simple as the time a person normally needs to formulate a response in a group discussion. "I didn't speak my mind in a group," Connie Gaines says, "if both men and women were discussing something." If she started to make a comment, "the men jumped in bing-bing-bing, and before I knew it the discussion was in another place, and I was still formulating my next thought."

Differences in communication style can lead to an unequal distribution of power because some persons end up having a greater voice in family discussions than others. Communication patterns distribute power in other ways as well. One of the most important concepts in family systems theory is "triangulation." In a triangle, one person (or subsystem) carries out a conflict with another person (or subsystem) through a third party. Simply by carrying the hostile messages from one person to another, the triangulated third party strengthens the power of the sender. Or consider what we call the "family switchboard" function. A family switchboard is a go-between who controls the flow of information between subsystems. Control of information is power; hence, switchboards become power brokers in the family system.

In this chapter we examine the relation between communication, power, and conflict in the family. One of our basic assumptions is that the relation between communication and power directly affects the family's ability to resolve conflicts. Distribution of power in the family governs family fights. Furthermore, if the distribution of power is perceived by some to be unfair, conflict will increase. People will begin to fight not only over the stated issues but over the power distribution itself.

Conflicts over power often take the form of "underground" fights. This inequality in power distribution is typically accompanied by rigid boundaries between church parents and children. In a family where the boundaries between parents and children tend toward rigidity (whether of the pure or mixed type), children often keep their conflicts with parents hidden. This may be due to fear of conflict with intimidating parents. It may also result from past failures to make themselves heard. Perhaps they tried to speak their minds but the parents repeatedly misunderstood or ignored them. The combination of dependent status and a rigid boundary encourages children to displace their conflict with parents by fighting among themselves. With the conflict focused among the children, there is no pressure on the parental boundary to open up. The conflict continues with little hope of resolution.

A systemic approach that focuses on modifying parental boundaries can restructure the system in a way that allows conflict management techniques a better chance of succeeding. Equally important, a systems approach aims to redistribute power in the family so that the family fights more fairly in all those everyday conflicts that can build to the point where a formal conflict management process becomes necessary.

Following are a variety of strategies for modifying boundaries as a way of addressing immediate church family conflicts and of changing the family system to handle conflict better in the future. The first of these strategies is foundational to the rest. It is to teach and reinforce certain rules of good communication and to do so in the midst of family life.

Teaching and Reinforcing Good Communication in the Family

There are many practices that promote good family communication in all settings.[1] Among the most important are the following:

1. Speak for yourself, not for someone else.
2. Don't interrupt.
3. Don't assume that other family members know what you are thinking or feeling if you haven't told them.
4. Avoid unqualified generalizations (never, no one, always, etc.).

Teaching and reinforcing the first rule is a key to modifying diffuse and rigid boundaries. Rigid boundaries have a chance of opening up and becoming permeable only when people communicate directly with one another. Diffuse boundaries become permeable when persons who are enmeshed begin to distinguish their own feelings and opinions from those of the person with whom they are enmeshed.

Let's imagine a pastor, whom we'll call Kathy Chambers, introducing the subject of improving communication in her church family by preaching a series of sermons that would touch at numerous points on communication patterns. One sermon, "Is Your Name Moses?" examines the partnership of Moses and Aaron described in Exodus 6:28–7:7. Because Moses is not a "good speaker," Aaron will speak for him to Pharaoh. With their different gifts, the two brothers will be a team in carrying out God's mission to captive Israel. But outside this special arrangement for mission, Aaron ought not to speak for Moses. Moses must speak for himself, sometimes even against his brother (Deut. 9:15-21).

Kathy asks the congregation to imagine Moses, Aaron, and other Israelite leaders having a meal together one evening in the wilderness. Aaron has been overdoing his assignment to be spokesman for Moses. As the group sits around a fire eating toasted manna, Aaron gives out Moses' opinion about the chances for rain, explains Moses' theory about where the pyramids came from, and defends Moses when anybody complains about how long it's taking to get to the promised land. And so it goes until Joshua, who has kept silence throughout the meal, asks whether Moses has an extra pair of sandals he might borrow. When Aaron begins to answer, Joshua asks, "Is your name Moses?"

Kathy uses the question, "Is your name Moses?" as a refrain in her sermon as she goes on to explain the difference between having the right to speak for others under certain circumstances and the responsibility of all to speak for themselves.

The following Thursday night at a board meeting, Kathy arrests any attempts by one person to speak for someone else by asking, with a smile, "Is your name Moses?" People laugh, and the point is made with grace. After that others begin using the question, Is your name Moses? to reinforce the first rule of good communication.

Creating a theme expressed by a metaphor that invites humor is a very effective way to teach in all pastoral situations. It helps to connect formal teaching and preaching with everyday communication events in the life of the church family. The pastor can weave a communication theme through a variety of settings, and if the metaphor is playful, others will begin to experiment with it, too, and will take over the work of upholding it.

Kathy is able to apply her metaphor spontaneously to a moment in a board meeting because she makes a habit of monitoring communication patterns in her church family. She pays attention especially to boundaries that are critical to family structure.

If her "map" tells her that a church conflict remains unresolved largely because two parents representing different subsystems have not learned to communicate well with each other, she can make a special point of focusing on the boundary between them. By the same token, monitoring patterns of communication is the way in which she gathers information in the first place about the nature and quality of the boundaries in the system.

Nurturing Parents and Children

Perhaps the most central parental figure at Grace Community Church is Palmer Hatch. He's also church moderator. Everyone likes Palmer, but he has a blustery way of exercising leadership that discourages more timid people from disagreeing openly with him. And their reluctance to oppose him is redoubled by their fondness for him. This is especially the case with many of the parental children, some of whom are on the Church Council. A number of these parental children have come to form a subsystem that pretty much does Palmer's bidding.

Every year Grace Church has a leadership retreat for the staff and members of the Church Council. The moderator and the pastor plan and lead this retreat as a team. This year Palmer has invited the Council to his new cottage on Crystal Lake. Pastor Allen Jeske and four members of the Council drive up together.

In the car on the way, the conversation turns to the agenda for the retreat, which is to include ministry envisioning for the coming year. Terry Larkin expresses concern that he doesn't want this year to be like last year, when "We worked out the church calendar, and then Palmer didn't follow through."

Allen knows that part of Terry's complaint is Terry's feeling that he doesn't get enough guidance from Palmer to carry out his own responsibilities. For example, when Terry was in charge of the All Church Picnic, Palmer told him, "We should have it after school gets out but before it gets too hot." That instruction frustrated Terry because Terry wanted to know when. That is, he wanted a date. The other members of the Council comment that Palmer is a "great guy," but "you can't always depend on him." Allen has heard most of this before and suggests that perhaps the retreat would be a good time to express some specific concerns to Palmer. The group agrees and discusses ways that planning and communication might be improved.

By noon they are at the cottage. Palmer ushers them into the backyard where he has been preparing a barbecue. They are greeted by a table laden with food in a corner of the yard shaded by gently swaying birch trees. Crystal Lake glitters merrily in the background. With his "family" gathered, Palmer invites the pastor to ask the blessing. Then all sit down to eat.

Allen knows that Terry and the others will never bring up the subject they talked about in the car, so he is looking for a chance to broach it tactfully. He finds an opportunity at the end of the meal. With everyone relaxing over coffee, Palmer declares, "I'm so glad we could all be together like this, and I hope that we can all get to know one another even better this weekend and learn to work together even better than before." Allen responds by expressing his agreement with Palmer and suggesting that there may be some things they all need to talk about this weekend.

"In fact," Allen continues, "the group was talking about some things on the way up that they'd like to discuss with you." "Oh?" says Palmer, with the beginnings of an injured look. "Well, what is it, Pastor?" Allen invites the group to speak for itself. Palmer echoes the pastor's invitation: "If you want to talk to me about something, go right ahead." But everyone can see the surprise and worry on his face. Terry interjects, "Well, I don't have any complaints." And the others offer that whatever problems there were last year aren't worth bringing up now.

Palmer looks relieved and says to Allen, with rising confidence, "Well, Pastor, you know that if there's anything on your mind you can certainly share it with me." Allen responds, "Well, I think the group needs to speak for itself, if there's anything they want to say." There is a moment of awkward silence. Then Janet Briscomb exclaims, "This is an absolutely beautiful setting, Palmer, and the lunch was delicious." Everyone chimes in with hearty agreement, and the next ten minutes are composed of comments about how lovely the surroundings are, how good the food was, and how kind it is of Palmer to open his summer retreat to the group.

What can Allen do? Let's imagine that later that afternoon, Allen draws Palmer aside and asks his assistance in a relationship-building exercise he has planned for the group. Palmer is eager to help. Part of their conversation might go as follows:

> *Palmer:* For me it's a question of learning to work as a team, with each one doing his part.
>
> *Allen:* Well, I knew you'd be supportive of anything we can do to strengthen our working relationships. Here's my concern. I don't think our leaders have learned to be as open with each other as they could be. We need to get more input in planning from Terry and Janet. I think sometimes they're holding back, that they just go along with me and you, when maybe they have different opinions—you know, just not to cause conflict. Do you ever get that feeling?

In these opening words Allen works to strengthen his affiliation with Palmer: asking for his help, using "we" and "me and you." In what follows Allen continues to affiliate with Palmer by expressing agreement with him, affirming him, and using "we" language throughout their conversation. He also avoids using the word "but." That is, he strengthens his efforts at affiliation by using a "Yes, and—" rather than a "Yes, but—" style of linking his points with Palmer's.

> *Palmer:* Well, I hadn't really thought about it, but if it's true, I certainly want to have everyone fully involved, get everyone's input.

Allen: I know you do. I think some don't give all their input because they don't want to hurt my feelings or your feelings when they disagree with us. I want to see if we can begin working this retreat on learning how to speak openly, disagree graciously, and discover that the world doesn't cave in if we have conflict.

Palmer: Well, I think we should just tell them to feel free to share any perspectives they have. Like I said at lunch.

Allen: I agree with you. I do think some of us have an easier time speaking our minds than others do. You remember that conversation we had in my office a couple months ago about including a regular "confession of sins" in the order of service?

Palmer: (*smiling*) Yes, I remember that conversation.

Allen: Yeah, we both got pretty angry. But I've never forgotten how that disagreement ended up. We cooled off, made some concessions to each other, shook hands, and you never let it affect our relationship after that. That impressed me very much—how good you seem to be at working through a conflict and then going on with kindness and grace.

This may be one of the few times in his life that Palmer did work through a conflict openly and gracefully. But Allen gives him the benefit of the doubt and holds up their "fight" as a model of good communication.

Allen: Do you think we could have another disagreement as a training exercise for the others to watch?

Palmer: You mean like a skit?

Allen: Exactly. But we won't tell them that until afterward. I was thinking we could stage a disagreement over dinner tonight, and then I'll use it as an object lesson for reflection at our 7:30 session, and we'll do some role plays with the group. Are you up for it?

Palmer: Yeah, I can do that.

Allen: I may want to include you in a role play with one of the others, too, like Terry.

Palmer: What are you and I going to argue about over dinner?

Allen: You help me pick the issue . . .

People learn best by imitating models, and modeling is often most effective when people understand that they are being shown models of how to do something. Allen enlists Palmer as a co-parent to help model good communication in a conflict. At the same time, Allen is nurturing Palmer as one parent to another. He draws Palmer's attention to one of their own conflicts as a model of how to disagree openly and graciously. The strategy of using a mock argument over dinner and role plays that evening is also directed toward Palmer himself. Instead of confronting Palmer directly with the fact that he has a problem in how he communicates with the group, Allen uses an indirect strategy that will allow him to coach Palmer without putting him on the defensive. The mock argument and role plays are only make-believe. All Palmer is asked to do is learn the role that the pastor teaches him to play.

In the role plays that evening, Allen has two goals: to help Palmer learn to listen to his "children" and to teach the parental children how to speak openly with Palmer as a step toward becoming co-parents with him. During the role play sessions, Allen will use his director-coach role to teach and reinforce rules of good communication. At this point, the "issues" that the participants fight about ought to be fictional. Terry and some of the others may find it difficult enough to play at open disagreement over imaginary issues. And Allen has an understanding with Palmer that what they are going to do is to playact. If this first evening goes well, perhaps tomorrow night the group will agree to some role plays around real issues.

Of course, Allen could bring up the group's issues himself in private with Palmer. Or he could name some of them as his own concerns at one of the dinner conversations. Allen could make it his pastoral duty to rescue family members whenever he thinks they are in difficulty or whenever they ask for help. But rescuing isn't nurture. To step in and do things for people that they should learn to do for themselves only reinforces their dependence.

It is significant that one of Terry's complaints about Palmer is that Palmer doesn't give him enough direction. Terry wants Palmer to be more paternalistic in the details of guidance. Fortunately, this is not Palmer's style. Allen can affirm Palmer for not being overly paternalistic and can encourage him to nurture Janet and Terry toward greater independence. If the boundary opens up a bit more between Palmer and the parental children, so that they can express some of their frustrations with him and he his frustrations with them, Palmer can probably do a pretty good job of "fathering" them into co-parenting roles. One of his complaints about them is that they don't "take hold of a job and get it done." Once he understands that they need support toward greater confidence in their own judgment and initiative, he will be better able to nurture them.

Blue Chips

At Fairfax United Methodist Church, Elwyn Carter, chair of the Christian Education Board, wants to find a playful way to encourage greater participation at board meetings. Let's imagine that at the beginning of a meeting he displays a stack of blue poker chips. Then he goes around the room and hands a chip to each of four persons (three women and one man). When he is finished, he sits down and says: "You know, I think I do too much talking at these meetings, so that some people here don't get a chance to get a word in. I think there are a few others of you like me that also tend to dominate our meetings. You have good ideas, so I understand why, but I would really like to hear from the four patient people to whom I've given the poker chips. So I'm going to introduce our first item of business, and no one else is allowed to speak until these four spend their chips by speaking first."

The four do speak, and then the group wants to talk about the game before going on. So Elwyn asks what they think the game meant. After a few moments of silence, Sheryl Anderson says, "I think some of us come to any discussion like this assuming we have a blue chip in our hand, or a fistful of blue chips. Others of us assume we don't have any blue chips."

A blue chip signifies a voice in family business and decision making. It is not an official voice but a family voice. And it is with good reason that we have imagined three of the four persons who received a blue chip from Elwyn being women. Research into gender differences between men and women in American society suggests that women are more apt than men to doubt whether they have something important to contribute to a group discussion when both men and women are present. For example, when July Fischer (recall chapter 6) is in a church family discussion, she assumes that what she might have to say is not important. Electing her to a church office does not change that assumption. She carries it with her, and other family members reinforce it. She has no blue chip.

But there is another reason why men tend to have more blue chips in the church family. It has to do with differences in communication style. Consider Sheryl Anderson. In a church family discussion, she wants to participate. But she never seems to be able to get into the flow of the talk if men are present. She has something to say and knows it, but she, too, has no blue chip.

After sitting through a meeting full of spoken and unspoken conflict, Sheryl goes home angry. She's not so much angry with those she strongly disagrees with. She's angry about the fact that she hardly participated in the discussion. And the one time she managed to say something, she was interrupted, only to watch the men take the conversation off in another direction: bing-bing-bing.

Several observations flowing out of research into differences in communication style between men and women help explain Sheryl's frustration.[2] These learnings are especially significant for understanding how power and authority become distributed in the church family in unequal ways that both create conflict and hinder conflict resolution.

First, in conversations between men and women, men tend to adopt the role of instructors and expect women to assume the role of passive listeners.[3] Second, men tend to speak more often and for longer lengths of time than women do in mixed group discussions.[4] And third, men move discussion at a pace that more women than men find uncomfortable.[5] Sometimes women say that the pace does not allow adequate time for digestion of one person's idea before someone immediately comments on it and the discussion rushes on.

The style of communication among men is typically aggressive. It treats discussion as a forum for staking out a position, emphasizing differences between one's own view and that of others. It means looking on arguments as something to win or lose. It also tends to be fast-paced. Those who cannot play this game well lose their public voice and thus forfeit an important avenue to acquiring family authority.

The typical style of communication among women is to seek points of similarity rather than difference. It means looking for ways to foster a feeling of connection rather than establishing one's own distinct position. It doesn't treat a discussion as a contest. And if a woman doesn't look upon a discussion as something to win, she is not likely to enter into it aggressively as a combatant. That explains in part why women tend not to be as forward in group discussion as men.

These differences tend to favor men's participation in family discussion and decision making. The so-called men's style is the preferred parental style in our churches. Those who adopt it are more likely to be regarded as parents than those who don't. That means that more men than women are likely to become parents in the church family. Which only reinforces the family assumption that the male style is the natural parental style.

Not all women tend toward the so-called women's style in communication; nor do all men tend toward the so-called men's style. We ought rather to imagine a continuum with people ranged all the way from one end to the other. Nevertheless, in our society men tend to cluster toward one end and women toward the other.

Today more and more women are rightfully aspiring to cross the official and unofficial parental boundaries that have typically represented a line of demarcation between them and men in American churches. The woman's role in the church has traditionally been limited to that of child or parental child. This has been especially true at the level of official structures. We think it has been less the case within the informal family systems, where more women have found parental roles when they were excluded from church offices. But even within the informal church family systems, males are privileged by tradition in their aspirations to parental status.

The unequal participation of family members in discussion and decision making is a systemic problem in church family communication. It crops up again and again at the very points where the church is supposed to be most democratic and inclusive. Where a gender hierarchy is present, women in a church family typically defer to men and remain passive in family business talk. Women with parenting ability often find it difficult to rise above the status of parental child. Or else they accept the role of parental child as appropriate for them.

Gender differences in communication tend to foster rigid boundaries between men and women in the church family. The rigid boundaries in turn reinforce the hierarchical pattern. Men don't discover the feelings and opinions of the women among them because communication is impaired and the implicit family rules say that "men generally know best" and ought to dominate the decision-making process.

Gender Differences and Family Conflict

As a consequence of hierarchies supported by gender differences in communication style, the dominant parents usually get their way without having to confront opposition from many of the children. Conflict is suppressed but not resolved.

This is especially true in a hierarchical family structure where there are rigid boundaries between male parents and female children. The parents typically act without thought to the opinions and feelings of the children. Often the parents assume that they already know what the children think or want. The children, for their part, don't possess habits of speaking their minds. Their styles of communication inhibit them in the presence of the parents.

In a hierarchical family, these rigid boundaries between men and women are often invisible, especially from the men's side, because the family rules don't require men to listen to women. Nor do family expectations encourage women to speak their minds or in some cases even to have their own opinions. The chief male parents therefore find it easy to presume that communication is taking place because they themselves are speaking clearly (or so they assume). Because the women rarely challenge male parental authority, the men assume that there is harmony and absence of conflict when in fact there may be considerable tension. The parental boundary may be conflicted at many points without the parents realizing it. As a consequence there is little hope of the conflicts being worked out.

Recall Steve Adams' explanation of why Margaret quit the choir at Belleville Baptist: "At the choir meeting she just said that the day she quit was 'the day a certain man came to sing in the choir who had never sung in the choir before,' and that just topped it off." Margaret complains to the other choir members and to the pastor about this, but she never says a word to the parent who put the man in the choir that morning: Bill. As a result the rigid boundary between Margaret and Bill is conflicted, but Bill is scarcely aware of it. And Margaret redirects her anger toward the pastor and the choir (other children). Placed within this larger family perspective, the so-called choir conflict cannot be resolved at a special meeting of the choir because a significant degree of the conflict flows out of the larger family system.

Helping Family Members Find Their Own Voices

In chapter 6 we imagined a planning team composed of Bruce Jenkins and July Fischer. Bruce assumes that other people should listen to him and follow his advice. July Fischer assumes that other people have better ideas than she does. If Bruce is a church parent, he is not one who can nurture July to greater self-confidence and independence. What can July's pastor, Larry Daniels, do to support her growth in the family?

First, Larry can go out of his way to affirm her contributions and especially any decisions in which she shows independence. This means that he must avoid giving her advice himself. If she asks him for advice, he can help her weigh options without giving his opinion. He can also express confidence in her wisdom to make decisions.

Second, and even more important for July's life in the church family, Larry can enlist other church parents to help nurture her. Instead of inviting her to work with a paternalistic parent like Bruce, Larry can pair her on the planning team with a parent who displays nurturing skills. Perhaps Connie Gaines is one of these. Given what Connie says about herself, as reported in the beginning of this chapter, she has learned to be more assertive in group settings with men like Bruce. Larry and Connie can strategize together about how Connie might nurture July toward greater self-confidence and independence.

Third, Larry must be careful not to ask family members like July to do everything. They are often persons who have difficulty saying no. In their desire to please they are often too willing to help. And in their lack of self-confidence, they often don't trust their own instincts when they "know" they should refuse a request. They may even become addicted to church work in their quest to feel needed and therefore valuable. (Recall the discussions of this subject in chapter 3.) Larry and others can support the chronic helpers who have low self-esteem by teaching them how to say no and praising them when they do so.

Spreading the Blue Chips

Sheryl Anderson doesn't need to find her own voice. She knows her mind. Her problem is that she has no blue chip to make her voice heard.

A starting point for seeing to it that Sheryl and other family members like her receive their fair share of blue chips is education about the differences that affect group communication. Pastors and church leaders can carry out such education in a variety of formats, utilizing any of the growing fund of resources available on inter-gender communication.

But education in traditional formats (preaching and class settings) will not lead to change unless the church family leaders actively practice techniques of making space for more family voices.

Those who preside over committee and board meetings, for example, can be trained to teach and reinforce communication rules designed to increase the participation. We will name three such rules.

The first rule is that no one is permitted to speak without receiving permission from the chair or group leader. This rule lays a foundation for a second. The privilege of speaking does not go to the first person who requests it (by raising a hand, etc.). This rule allows the group leader the discretion to pass over those who always have something to say (and who think of it immediately, perhaps sometimes without adequate reflection) and to give the floor to the less aggressive members. The third rule is to allow more time between comments. This slows down the pace of the discussion and encourages wider participation. Once otherwise reticent persons adopt the habit of participating, the pause between comments may be shortened.

Group leaders who use these rules can also increase participation by being certain to ask those who have not spoken for their opinion. This not only gives them the opportunity to speak, which they might not otherwise have taken, it also sends an important message: that their voice counts.

Another strategy for increasing participation is to designate someone (other than the person leading the meeting) as communication monitor. The job of such a monitor is to keep track of who participates, how often, and how long. The monitor has the right to interrupt someone who has been dominating the discussion and to point out when some are being left out. If the monitor is to function effectively, the group itself must grant the monitor permission to hold both individuals and the group as a whole to accountability for the fairness and inclusiveness of the process.

Pastors who make it part of their care for the family system to train church leaders in group communication skills should also be very liberal in affirming everyone's efforts to put such skills into practice. That means praising people not only for the business they accomplish but also for the quality of communication they foster.

The Power of Family Memory

Communication in the church family takes place not only among the living. There is often a continuing communication with family members from the past as well. Guardians of the family memory control communications with dead parents.

Since family history is profoundly definitive of family identity, the person who controls the information about the past has a great deal of authority in shaping current family identity. And because identity influences practice, the keeper of the family memory has considerable power in any planning and decision-making process.

"We have never done it that way," says Mr. Memory. In fact, the church has done it "that way"—or at least in similar ways—in the past, but no one remembers and no one questions Mr. Memory's assertion, much less his exclusive right to make such assertions. Even if others remember it differently, they don't say so, because Mr. Memory has family authority when it comes to the past.

It is our view that the family history belongs to the church family as a whole, even to newer members who have participated in very little of it themselves. All have a right to speak about the past as they remember it or are able to reconstruct it. If a Mr. or Ms. Memory is using appeals to the past in a paternalistic way, his or her exclusive claims to the family memory can be challenged in a variety of ways.

First, when Mr. Memory speaks about the past, the pastor or one of the other parents can say, "Bob [Mr. Memory] has said something very significant. We should consider the ways in which the church has handled this kind of question in the past. I'm sure there is something to be learned there. Let's do some investigation and see what we can discover."

As the "we" in this example suggests, the way to deprive Mr. Memory of exclusive ownership of the family memory is to get other family members to reclaim the past. An invitation for numerous people to share their memories at church anniversaries and other occasions is one strategy. Including recent members with recent memories is especially important during such collective remembering because it signals everyone's share in the growing family memory.

A response to Mr. Memory by saying, "Let's do some investigation," suggests another strategy for redistributing the family memory. Enlisting a group of people in some modest or extensive historical research into the past can help spread the authority of memory to others in the family. Often the family history turns out to be much different from what we assume, especially when our assumptions are based on what the exclusive guardians of the family memory have been telling us. When the work of such a historical task force is completed, each member of the team should be encouraged to share in reporting the results, so that the practice of numerous voices speaking about the past becomes established.

Rewiring Communications Systems: Triangles and Switchboards

A Mr. Memory is a kind of mediator between the living church family and its past. But there are also other forms of mediation in church family communication. Two of the most important kinds are triangulation and what we term the "switchboard" function.

The form of triangulation on which we will focus here occurs when one person fights with another person through a third party. Typically it also means that the other person fights back through the "triangulated" third party.

The triangulated person is in a very vulnerable position. Both sides demand that the person they've placed in the middle take sides with them. When the triangulated person sides with one and the other person finds out, the other interprets that as a betrayal.

Third parties often get drawn unsuspectingly into triangulated communications. But some people like to serve as "go-betweens" because it puts them in charge of family information. As we have noted, control of information in the church is a form of power. Some people make it their business to create triangles in which they are always the third party. They weave a network of communication lines in which they are the central switchboard.

For example, if Adelle is in the habit of speaking for Mary, the communication between Mary and any other subsystems will suffer. The boundary between Mary and others will become rigid. And if Adelle has acquired the role of go-between in a number of relationships within the system, then she is functioning as a "switchboard." The boundary between her and others may be open, but the boundaries between the systems she mediates are closed.

The switchboard function is to be clearly distinguished from occasional and shared help from others in communication. Many communications need mediation. But the switchboard function is chronic mediation. Instead of helping to create and maintain permeable boundaries, switchboards interpose themselves between subsystems, thus cutting off direct communication.

By controlling more than their own communications, switchboards acquire unfair power in the family system. They can modify a message by editing it, enhancing it, changing its tone, or commenting on it. They may even invent communications by reporting something that wasn't said or by claiming that "people are saying . . ." when it is only they themselves who are doing the saying.

A switchboard may be a gossip, who loves the experience of power that comes with sharing information. A switchboard may also be a well-meaning mediator, who takes over the role of communicating another person's feelings to others. Or a switchboard may be a manipulator, who withholds and dispenses information in a calculated way in order to gain more power in the system.

By making others indebted to them for family information, manipulative switchboards sometimes manage to convert the power that comes with their role into authority. And those without authority can acquire considerable power by cultivating a switchboard function for themselves. Thus switchboards can be found either above or below the parental boundary.

Teaching and reinforcing the rules of good communication is the basic strategy for dismantling triangles and eliminating family switchboard functions. In the case of invitations to triangulation, this means teaching family members a strategy of response such as the following: (1) refuse to take a message from one person to another; (2) tell those who share the "problems" they are having with others to go speak to the other person directly; and (3) refuse to listen to them if they don't practice this form of direct communication. Imagine Janet practicing this response with Terry:

Terry: Janet, you're not going to believe what Palmer said to me last night.

Janet: I probably will believe, but don't tell me. First I want to know, did you tell him how you felt about whatever it was?

Terry: No, it caught me off guard.

Janet: Well, I don't feel comfortable talking to you about it until you first talk to Palmer. If you want, I'll go with you, and I'll give you moral support, but you have to speak to him for yourself.

Terry: Can't I just tell you what he said?

Janet: No, I don't feel right about it. All we do is talk about Palmer behind his back. And half the time I end up going to Pastor about something that happened with you and Palmer. I just don't feel comfortable doing that any more. As I said, when you're ready to talk with Palmer, I'll go with you, if you want. We can have lunch with him or something. But right now let's talk about something else.

Janet is not refusing to talk about Palmer with Terry under any circumstances. She is resisting the pattern that makes her the mediator between the two of them.

Unlike those who get triangulated, persons in switchboard roles will typically resist advice about how to give up their function as go-between, because loss of their switchboard role deprives them of considerable power. Nevertheless, switchboards cannot stay in operation without lines coming in. Teaching people to communicate directly with one another means teaching them not to plug into a switchboard when they have something to say to someone else.

The Pastor as Switchboard

As persons to whom people are constantly bringing information and concerns about the church family, pastors can easily fall into the trap of assuming switchboard functions. Take Jeannette Sears, associate pastor at First Congregational Church of Blue Lake. Because Jeannette was a "people person" and because she had the trust of almost everyone in the church, many of whom were longtime friends, she discovered that she was often in the middle of things. In fact, she liked to take care of things for people, and she enjoyed acting as a mediator. Until it started causing her trouble.

Upon reflecting about her ministry style from a systems perspective, Jeannette realized that she had not only allowed but also encouraged triangles to form in which she was the third-party go-between. She also discerned that her tendency to get "triangulated" was related to an aspect of her communication style. She liked to speak for others. Sometimes speaking for others meant explaining them or defending them to someone else. Sometimes it meant that in a group situation Jeannette would dominate discussions with comments and suggestions. She didn't realize that this, too, was a form of speaking for others until she tried an experiment. She scaled back her verbal participation in committee meetings and discovered that other people (other women, in fact) began making many of the same observations and suggestions that she would otherwise have made. She realized that in the past she'd been jumping in ahead of them and, in effect, usurping their right and obligation to establish their own voices in the family.

By changing her own style of communication, Jeannette "rewired" the communications system in the congregation at a strategic point. Simply by modifying her own patterns of communication in the family, she precipitated a restructuring of the system. People could no longer go through her to speak to (or get at) someone else. Nor could people depend on her to "say everything that needed to be said." This compelled others to assume more responsibility and to move out of dependent roles (as parental children) into parent roles. Jeannette lost some of her own power in the system, but she also extricated herself from the very vulnerable position of being the third party in many triangles. And she helped others to grow up.

Jeannette Sears not only worked herself out of being a switchboard, she also began teaching and reinforcing the basic rules of good family communication in both formal and informal family settings. And she made it one of her central ministry goals to teach other parents in her church family to do the same. But Jeannette is no longer at Blue Lake.

As Jeannette tells her story, Owen Masters, senior pastor, had already decided that she had too much influence in the church. He resented the fact that she had the ear of so many in the congregation and decided to have her fired before she was politically in a stronger position than he. Owen succeeded, by using what Jeannette described as unfair tactics, including violations of confidence.

After looking back on what happened, Jeannette concludes that both she and Owen had been playing games to increase their own personal power in the family. Not that either of them would have admitted that. She knows that she herself had always been able to rationalize that whatever she did to help people was in the best interests of the church, whatever its effects on Owen's status in the church.

In the end Jeannette lost the power game, ironically just when she'd started playing by a different set of rules. Today she is pastor of another church, where she makes it one of her central ministry goals to teach other parents in her church family to practice and reinforce rules of communication that open up boundaries and distribute blue chips to all. Her new family hasn't mastered this new game yet. They're still learning. So is Jeannette.

Chapter Eight

❖

Joining

We have followed the story of Pastor Steve Adams and the Belleville Baptist Church family throughout this study, and in chapter 5 we mapped Steve's congregation from the standpoint of a conflict in the church choir. A very active choir member named Margaret had quit, and Steve was afraid the choir was falling apart. So he called a "re-organizational" meeting that deteriorated into a fight, leaving Steve "on the sidelines" watching the conflict but unable to lead the meeting. "It was impossible to parent in that situation," Steve later reflected. But he admitted that had Bill Lewis been present, Bill could have parented.

Bill is the central parent in the Belleville church family. In fact, in the interim between the departure of the former pastor and the arrival of Steve, Bill assumed a variety of pastoral functions, thus enlarging his parental role.

Bill is a heavy-handed parent who shows little sensitivity to the feelings of others. He imposes his will on his congregational children: making them listen to hours of taped radio preaching on a Wednesday night when Steve is absent, directing a distraught visitor to sing in the choir without notice on a Sunday morning, dictating to the nominating committee (of which he is not a member), even telling the pastor when to pray. Of course, church members are not obliged to do what Bill says. But generally they do, because he is their parent.

Once he recognized the role of Bill in the Belleville church family and the way in which Bill was involved in the choir conflict, Steve began to devise some strategies to modify his church family system. As a result he succeeded in clarifying and strengthening his own pastoral role, but throughout the remainder of his time at Belleville he never achieved parental status in the church family. There are no doubt several reasons for this, but we are going to focus on only one: the possibility that Steve never *joined* the Belleville family.

Joining Through Affirmation and Identification

All who participate in the life of the congregation belong to the family in some way. But it is possible for one to remain only marginally related to the family, with the result that it is never clear whether one really belongs or not.

In chapter 1 we told the story of a young pastor treated by his church like a foster child who finds himself in a family that makes it clear he doesn't really belong. A newcomer cannot join without invitations and acceptance by the family, especially the parents. But joining itself is something the newcomer must decide to do. Churches have explicit rituals by which new members and new pastors join their official ranks. Joining the church family is another matter. It has its own rules, but they are nowhere written down. And there are no official ceremonies that establish whether one is in or out.

The best way to understand how one joins the church family is by seeing it as a kind of affiliation strategy. New-comers aren't born into the church family. As a rule they become integrated family members only be responding to the family's invitations to join. That response must include at least two elements of affiliation: affirmation and identification.

Affirmation means expressing appreciation and praise to others for the things we value about them. Identification means discovering and matching similarities between ourselves and others. As a strategy of joining, identification also means adopting the ways of the family.

Several of Steve's descriptions suggest that he feels ashamed to be pastor of Belleville. Listen to what he says about the choir. "You have some people screaming at the top of their lungs and some aren't singing at all. . . . The repertoire is about ten country-and-western songs, gospel songs, which they recycle regularly." He shakes his head.

Do the people feel the same way? "No!" Steve exclaims. "They think the choir's just great. They get tears in their eyes every Sunday when the choir sings 'Beulah Land' or whatever."

Then there's Bill, with his tapes of fundamentalist radio preachers and other habits that embarrass Steve. Steve describes him as "slick." But what do the people think of Bill? "Oh!" Steve says, mocking how church members speak of Bill, "we just love Bill." "He's the greatest." "If it wasn't for Bill the church wouldn't be here."

Why do people feel this way about Bill? "He gives the people a lot of attention," Steve explains, "a tremendous amount of attention." But in Steve's judgment Bill is a permissive parent, giving without making any demands. Sometimes he makes people angry, but most of the time he makes them feel good.

And how do the people experience Steve? How does Steve make them feel? "Frustrated," Steve says. "There aren't connections." In fact, Denise once told Steve, "You make me feel like I'm not a Christian."

Bill accepts the people as they are. He doesn't try to change them or "fix" them. He likes the choir and is vocal in praising it. He even attends rehearsals (although he doesn't sing). He gives everyone a lot of attention. Steve preaches about the church's responsibility to confront racism and poverty. He is constantly working to improve the quality of worship. At the same time, he confesses that he would never invite any of his friends to visit Belleville. He's too ashamed. "Sometimes the place is like a zoo," Steve says, summing up his worst feelings about the congregation. One can hardly doubt that the church senses this. And Steve confirms that his efforts to improve the quality of congregational life and ministry are often taken as attacks. "For example," Steve recalls, "they interpreted the announcement in the bulletin about the reorganizational meeting of the choir as being hateful."

Hateful is a strong word. One suspects that the people are having difficulty distinguishing Steve's prophetic appeals and efforts to change things at Belleville from the unspoken message that he doesn't really like them or wish to be identified with them. Which raises the question of whether a pastor can carry on a prophetic ministry without first emphatically joining the church family.

We think it is an unspoken rule of most church families that the pastor's right to be heard as a prophet depends on the pastor's having first joined the family through clear acts of affirmation and identification. If Steve has joined Belleville, he has done so in only tentative ways and with mixed signals. His prophetic preaching is not accepted by the family because Steve hasn't earned the right as a family member to speak about the sins of the family. Viewed from the standpoint of "joining," we would guess that Steve's dissociation of himself from Bill only encourages the family to treat Steve as a marginal family member. He asserts himself pastorally in ways that they'll accept only from a parent, but in their eyes his status in the family is probably that of an independent child who has not yet decided to join them.

Joining the Belleville family thus appears to be the strategy of greatest importance and urgency for Steve. But he must be honest with himself. Perhaps he isn't willing to join this family. In effect that's what Steve eventually decided. A year after the incident with the choir, Steve accepted a call from another church.

The Christmas Hat

Let's imagine an effective effort to join a church family. Three weeks into his pastorate at Silver Ridge United Methodist Church in Cheyenne, Wyoming, Pastor Kent Harrison purchases a pair of cowboy boots to wear to the church's annual October hoedown. Kent is from the East. He has never owned cowboy boots, never liked Western music all that much, and doesn't know how to dance a hoedown. But he is determined to cultivate a taste for all the local culture of his new church family. The cowboy boots are a hit. And that Christmas, one of the parishioners presents him with a ten-gallon hat.

Kent brings his new hat into the pulpit at the Christmas Eve service and uses it as a prop in his sermon. He begins by making a few jokes at his own expense about himself and the hat. Then he comments that the first people God invited to see the Christ child were people of the land, who lived with the sky and the earth. The shepherds would have loved a hat like the one he'd gotten for Christmas, to keep the sun from "smiting them by day."

Kent goes on to tell a story about a pioneer couple traveling west across America in the 1830s. A child was born to them along the way, and having little to keep it warm, they wrapped it in a scarf and tucked it into the man's great hat, the way Miriam sheltered Moses in the basket among the bullrushes and the way Joseph and Mary nestled the infant Jesus in a rustic manger.

God shows up in common places, Kent says. God gives Christ to the common people of the earth and especially to the poor. And although Mary, Joseph, and the shepherds did not conclude that they were better than others because Christ came first to them, they did learn the wondrous fact that God is no respecter of persons but loves all alike. The birth of the Christ child in a common place is a sign of that. Christ joined Joseph and Mary along the road, Christ became a member of their family at a moment when they had no place to go. This is what "Immanuel" means. "God is with us," they could say, "because Christ joined us when we had no place to go and no bed to offer him except a trough used to feed the animals." And if you remember that, Kent says, you will understand how far the promise reaches when God says, "I will never leave you or forsake you."

"God loves us," Kent continues, "just as God loved Mary, Joseph, and those shepherds. This Christmas, God is pleased to dwell with us, right where God finds us." And with these words, Kent leaves the pulpit to place the hat on the communion table. Then he smiles and tells the people, "Christ is born to us this night and is happy to sleep here in this big hat. It is a sign that God is with us, right here in Cheyenne. Christ is happy to be a Wyoming baby this night, to let us know the wonder of God's love for us."

Kent's sermon carries two messages bound together. One is that God loves and accepts the people of Silver Ridge United Methodist Church. The other is that Kent himself can celebrate God's incarnation in the trappings of traditional Cheyenne tradition, which means that Kent wills to join the Silver Ridge church family. And this second, unspoken message becomes the vehicle for communicating the first, explicit message. Kent is the newcomer, the man from the culturally alien East. By extending the call, the church has said that it accepts him; and by consenting to come, Kent has said that he accepts the church. But there are still many open questions. Will he really accept them as they are? The Christmas Eve sermon offers one more affirmation in a series of powerful symbolic responses that Kent has been giving to that question ever since he arrived in September. Those responses communicate that he does accept them and wants to join them just as they are. Because Kent continually interweaves his own joining maneuvers with the explicit message of God's love and acceptance toward the congregation, Kent's acts of joining also become symbols of God's embrace of the church family.

But it is not only the pastor who can carry such incarnate messages to the church family. Any family member can be the bearer of such a message. It is one of the ironies of the family stories we have told that the man who is arguably the worst parent of all, Bill Lewis, manages to become a voice for God's unconditional acceptance at Belleville Baptist, while the pastor, Steve Adams, for all his sound theology and good intent, fails to get this message across because he cannot bring himself to join the family. He thinks he's in some kind of a "zoo." Which translates, I don't belong here at all.

Joining Is an Act of Faith

Sometimes churches prefer to keep pastors in the box of the ministerial office and accord them only a marginal place in the family. Sometimes pastors prefer to confine their identification with the church, as far as possible, to their identity in the pastoral office. Outside of the pastoral office, they seek a place on the outskirts of the church family. But we have seen that the pastor who does not become a parent in the family is in a very weak position from which to handle congregational conflict and to participate effectively in church decision making. Not only that, there is also a profoundly Christian question linked with the otherwise strategic matter of joining, as Kent Harrison's sermon shows. To be imitators of God we must join the church family just as God does.

Ministering without joining the family makes the pastorate a professional activity at odds with the way of Christ and the Spirit. The Spirit forms the family of God out of nothing other than the familylike social group that the congregation concretely is. There is no spiritual "family of God" distinct from the social entity we have been describing as the familylike church. The spiritual church is the familylike social organization being led by the Spirit of God. To join the church family is to join those whom the Spirit has adopted as children of God. To reject the familylike social system is to reject implicitly the very stuff out of which the Spirit creates the divine household.

Pastors who resist joining the church families to which they minister disqualify themselves as bearers of the fundamental truth of spiritual adoption, the deepest message of Christ's incarnational appearance. By not accepting birth "in a manger" or "in a hat"—or whatever the local symbol may be—they locate themselves on the boundary of their church family. From that point of distance, it is almost impossible for them to speak God's words of love and acceptance in a convincing way. And pastors who take up a prophetic stance on the margins of the family are likely to confront a wall of resistance, because the family itself has not granted them the right to name the family sins and help chart the family destiny.

Those who do not join but seek the boundary of the family, where one is really neither "in" nor "out," discover that ministry can easily turn into the mere application of "techniques," none of which "work," because those on the boundary have neither the power nor the authority in the family to use techniques effectively. That goes for the techniques presented in this book as well. Only those who have joined their church family will be able to use family systems methods fruitfully.

Joining need not take the form of an immersion in which the congregation becomes the all-consuming world for the pastor. In fact, it is important that the pastor have membership in other systems apart from the church family in order to preserve enough independence from the congregational system to analyze it objectively and act within it in creative ways. Sometimes a pastor's nuclear family can serve as an outside system. But pastoral families are typically part of the church family system and therefore usually cannot provide a sufficient base of independence for the pastor. Collegial support groups can often supply not only emotional support for a pastor in times of difficulty but also valuable outside interpretations of oneself and one's church family system. And we recommend using this book with one or more colleagues in such a support group if that is possible.

"Joining," like all the other strategies we have described, is not a procedure that one can carry out mechanically. It is "more an attitude than a technique," as Minuchin says.[1] Some church families are easy to join. Others are not. It requires an act of faith to join a church family, whether that faith takes the form of buoyant confidence about embracing people who seem to be "just like me" or is a kind of courage in joining what looks to be more like a "zoo" than a family.

Usually the church does not appear to us in either of these two extremes but as some mixture of people who are both like and unlike us, as well as both likable and unlikable from our point of view. The technique of joining emphasizes the like and the likable in moves of affirmation and identification. Faith in joining means trusting that the Spirit has already made the church family God's own family. It means believing that the Christ child is really born into ordinary families and under all the common and odd circumstances that make up ordinary family life.

Of these two, faith is the more important; technique is secondary. And therefore we offer the techniques presented in this book as just one more tool by which those who have faith may help God's local families to "grow up" and live more faithfully as bearers of the new humanity in Christ.

Notes

PREFACE

1. A first effort to apply this insight is Dennis D. Hatfield, "A Model for Pastoral Ministry: Utilizing the Family Systems Therapy of Salvador Minuchin and the Theology of St. Paul" (D.Min. thesis; Northern Baptist Theological Seminary, 1986).

2. See Alan S. Gurman, David P. Kniskern, and William M. Pinsof, "Research on the Process and Outcome of Marital and Family Therapy," in *Handbook of Psychotherapy and Behavior Change*, 3rd ed., ed. Sol L. Garfield and Allen E. Bergin (New York: John Wiley & Sons, 1986), p. 606.

3. There have been at least two broad applications of systems theory to pastoral leadership and administration. See E. Mansell Pattison, *Pastor and Parish—A Systems Approach* (Philadelphia: Fortress Press, 1977) and Alvin J. Lindgren and Norman Shawchuck, *Management for Your Church* (Nashville: Abingdon, 1977). These books are very useful, but it is not their purpose to employ family systems theory to the local congregation as familylike in structure and process.

4. Edwin H. Friedman, *Generation to Generation: Family Process in Church and Synagogue* (New York and London: Guilford, 1985).

5. Kenneth R. Mitchell, *Multiple Staff Ministries* (Louisville: Westminster Press, 1988). Although Mitchell focuses on staff relations, he also gives some attention to ways in which family systems theory illuminates the larger systemic dynamics of the congregation as a whole.

6. We have relied especially on the following two books by Minuchin: *Families and Family Therapy* (Cambridge, Mass.: Harvard University Press, 1974) and *Family Therapy Techniques*, with Charles H. Fishman (Harvard University Press, 1981).

7. *Conjoint Family Therapy*, rev. ed. (Palo Alto, Calif.: Science and Behavior Books, 1967); *Peoplemaking* (Science and Behavior Books, 1972).

8. See the literature cited in notes 3, 4, and 5. We also recommend the use of other systems approaches.

9. For an exploration of the "family dynamics" of Roman Catholic church life, see Virginia Curran Hoffman, *Codependent Church* (New York: Crossroad, 1991).

10. We are using the categories presented by Lyle E. Schaller, *Looking in the Mirror: Self-Appraisal in the Local Church* (Nashville: Abingdon Press, 1984), 16. In the last ten years Schaller has expanded his definition of the

large church to represent congregations with more than 400 in worship attendance, and he has added the very large, seven-day-a-week church to represent congregations with more than 1,000 members.

11. We do not wish to overstate this or over-generalize. A helpful study of such differences is Thomas Kochman, *Black and White Styles in Conflict* (Chicago and London: University of Chicago Press, 1981).

12. For a discussion of pastoral authority in the black church, see Floyd Massey, Jr., and Samuel Barry McKinney, *Church Administration in the Black Perspective* (Valley Forge, Pa.: Judson Press, 1976).

ONE: WE'RE BUILDING YOU A HOUSE

1. *Peoplemaking* (Palo Alto, Calif.: Science and Behavior Books, 1972), 290.

2. M. Scott Peck, *People of the Lie: The Hope for Healing Human Evil* (New York: Simon and Schuster, 1983), 223.

3. Dietrich Bonhoeffer stressed this in his book, *The Communion of Saints: A Dogmatic Inquiry into the Sociology of the Church* (New York and Evanston: Harper & Row, 1963), where he inaugurated a theological approach to the church through the lens of sociology. According to Bonhoeffer, "Every genuinely theological concept can be correctly comprehended only when set within and supplemented by its special social sphere" (from the preface).

4. Wayne A. Meeks, *The First Urban Christians: The Social World of the Apostle Paul* (New Haven and London: Yale University Press, 1983), 84.

5. See Rom. 16:5; 1 Cor. 1:11; 16:15, 19; Col. 4:15; Philem. 2; and 2 John 10.

6. Gal. 6:10 ("household of faith"); 1 Pet. 2:5 ("a spiritual house"); 1 Tim. 3:15 ("the household of God"; so also 1 Pet. 4:17 and Eph. 2:19).

7. For a history of family systems theory and practice, see William C. Nichols and Craig A. Everett, *Systemic Family Therapy: An Integrative Approach* (New York and London: Guilford, 1986), 1-63.

8. See Edwin H. Friedman, *Generation to Generation: Family Process in Church and Synagogue* (New York and London: Guilford, 1985), chap. 8.

9. Kenneth C. Haugk, *Antagonists in the Church: How to Identify and Deal with Destructive Conflict* (Minneapolis: Augsburg Publishing House, 1988), 39.

TWO: CHURCH FAMILY STRUCTURE

1. The reason for this is that the diffuse boundary always forms out of an entrenched tendency of a personality toward enmeshment, while rigid boundaries can form for a variety of reasons, many of which are easy to counteract.

2. Salvador Minuchin, *Families and Family Therapy* (Cambridge, Mass.: Harvard University Press, 1974), 53.

3. Ibid., 97.

THREE: CHURCH FAMILY AUTHORITY

1. Richard Sennett, *Authority* (New York: Alfred Knopf, 1980). Our attention was drawn to Sennett's study by Letty M. Russell's excellent book, *Household of Freedom: Authority in Feminist Theology* (Philadelphia: Westminster Press, 1987).

2. Quoted from Abraham Zaleznik, "The Dynamics of Subordinacy," *Harvard Business Review* 43/3 (1965): 123-24.

3. Sennett comments that the Blackman-Dodds case study has been frequently cited in management circles as a model of how an employer should handle a demanding employee (*Authority*, 97).

4. On co-dependence and its predominance among women, see Anne Wilson Shaef, *Co-Dependence: Misunderstood—Mistreated* (San Francisco: Harper & Row, 1986). On the significance of the category of co-dependence for what we are defining as maternalism, see esp. pp. 34-47 (co-dependence and the women's movement), 44-47 (co-dependence and enmeshment), and 52, 56 (control issues and caregiving).

5. On this syndrome, see the illuminating analysis by Virginia Curran Hoffman, *The Co-Dependent Church* (Crossroad: New York, 1991).

6. In describing Harriet Walter's understanding of her own identity as a hindrance to her own "self-formation," we are relying especially on the work of modern feminist theorists, such as Anne Wilson Schaef 's *Women's Reality* (see n. 2 to chap. 7). An early and highly influential theological essay on this subject is Valerie Saiving Goldstein's "The Human Situation: A Feminine View," *Journal of Religion* 40 (1960): 100-112.

7. In situations where family authority is not divided up according to gender, one may speak of "simply parental" authority. Whether such situations yet exist even in our time is debatable.

FOUR: FAMILY RULES AND GAMES

1. Eric Berne, *Games People Play: The Psychology of Human Relationships* (New York: Grove Press, 1964).

FIVE: MAPPING

1. Henry Fielding, *Rape Upon Rape*, II.V.

2. Steve called the special choir meeting but then discovered that he couldn't take charge: "I felt very helpless. . . . I was trying to be a parent, I think, except I had—I couldn't do it. It was impossible to parent." This last statement is only relatively true. If Bill had been present, Bill could have parented.

3. A more precise description of affiliation can be found in chapter 5.

4. Note that parent to parent is not a parental relation.

SIX: CHANGING THE HIDDEN SYSTEM: FOCUSED STRATEGIES

1. We have derived these axioms from Minuchin's corpus in general and have adapted them to the congregation as a family system. See, e.g., Minuchin, *Families and Family Therapy* (Cambridge, Mass.: Harvard University Press, 1974), 9.

2. See, e.g., the last chapter of Minuchin and Fishman, *Family Therapy Techniques* (Cambridge, Mass.: Harvard University Press, 1981).

SEVEN: SPREADING THE BLUE CHIPS: COMMUNICATION AND POWER

1. Among the many books on interpersonal communication, Virginia Satir's *Conjoint Family Therapy* (Palo Alto, Calif.: Science and Behavior Books, 1967), to which we have already referred, remains an excellent guide.

2. For an excellent and highly readable introduction, see Deborah Tannen, *You Just Don't Understand: Women and Men in Conversation* (New York: Ballantine, 1990). A related, ground-breaking work is Anne Wilson Schaef, *Women's Reality: An Emerging Female System in the White Male Society* (Minneapolis: Winston, 1981).

3. See Tannen, *You Just Don't Understand*, chap. 5.

4. Ibid., 75-76, based on a study by Barbara and Gene Eakins, as well as one by Marjorie Swacker. But anyone can verify these findings by keeping track of men's and women's participation in any mixed group discussion of an issue.

5. We base this on what women have told us. See also the confirming judgment of Tannen, *You Just Don't Understand*, 87-88.

EIGHT: JOINING

1. *Family Therapy Techniques* (Cambridge, Mass.: Harvard University Press, 1981), 31.

Glossary

❖

child: One who typically defers to the judgment of others (parents or parental children) in church family decision-making processes.

coalition: When two or more persons or subsystems unite against another person or subsystem.

diffuse boundary: A boundary quality (associated with enmeshment) indicating that thoughts and feelings are flowing back and forth between two persons or subsystems but in a way that does not make it clear whose thoughts and feelings belong to whom.

independent child: One who makes up his or her own mind in family decision-making processes but to whom no other children defer.

parent: One to whom others defer in church family decision-making processes.

parental boundary: The unofficial division between parents and children indicating who (those "above the line") exercises unofficial authority in the family.

parental child: One to whom some children defer but who typically defers to one or more parents in family decision-making processes, especially important ones.

parity boundary: A boundary between persons or subsystems of relatively equal authority (parent to parent, child to child, etc.).

porous boundary: A boundary quality indicating interaction that is frequent enough and clear enough for two persons or subsystems to understand one another (also called an "open" or "permeable" boundary).

rigid boundary: A boundary quality indicating interaction that is not frequent enough or clear enough for mutual understanding to occur between two persons or subsystems (also called a "closed" boundary).

triangle/triangulation: A relationship in which two parties communicate through a third party.

Note: Every boundary must be defined in terms of both its nature (parental or parity) and quality (porous, rigid, or diffuse). Boundaries can also be "mixed" (e.g., a person who tends toward enmeshment in relationship with one who tends toward autonomy) or "disputed" (e.g., when one parent treats another parent like a child). Location "above" the parental boundary is not a reflection of emotional maturity. It indicates that one possesses family authority, whether or not one uses it in mature and up-building ways. And holding a church "office" does not in itself mean that one is a parent in the *family* system. A boundary between a parental child and his or her children is drawn horizontally. All parity boundaries are drawn vertically.